# Reading, Writing and Reasoning: A Guide for Students

SRHE and Open University Press imprint
*General Editor:* Heather Eggins

*Current titles include:*

# Reading, Writing and Reasoning: A Guide for Students

Gavin J. Fairbairn
Christopher Winch

The Society for Research into Higher Education
& Open University Press

Published by SRHE and
Open University Press
Celtic Court
22 Ballmoor
Buckingham
MK18 1XW

and
1900 Frost Road, Suite 101
Bristol, PA 19007, USA

First Published 1991
Reprinted 1992, 1993 (twice), 1995, 1996

*British Library Cataloguing in Publication Data*

Fairbairn, Gavin J.
  Reading, writing and reasoning: a guide for
  students.
  I. Title.   II. Winch, Christopher
  428

  ISBN 0–335–09596–8
  ISBN 0–335–09595–X (pbk)

*Library of Congress Cataloging-in-Publication Data*

Fairbairn, Gavin.
    Reading, writing and reasoning: a guide for students/Gavin J.
    Fairbairn, Christopher Winch.
      p.    cm.
    Includes bibliographical references (p. ) and index.
    ISBN 0–335–09596–8      ISBN 0–335–09595–X (pbk.)
    1. Study, Method of.   2. Reading (Higher education)
    3. English language–style.   4. Thought and thinking–study and teaching
    (Higher)   5. Reasoning–study and teaching (Higher)
    I. Winch, Christopher.   II. Title.
    LB2395.F28   1991
    428.4′071′1 – dc20                                          91–14734 CIP

Typeset by Type Study, Scarborough
Printed in Great Britain by St Edmundsbury Press Limited
Bury St Edmunds, Suffolk

# Contents

## Part 3: Developing Coherent Trains of Thought

# Preface and Acknowledgements

Most students will have to write essays at some time or another. For students of disciplines such as philosophy, politics and literature, most of the assessments to which they are subjected will take the form of essays whether these are written over an extended period or in a limited time within an examination hall. Because of this it is worth spending considerable effort in developing the skills necessary to write successfully. Our reason for deciding to write this book was that we were disturbed by the lack of skill intelligent students often seemed to demonstrate in writing essays for us. No matter how articulate they were in class there always seemed to be a large proportion of students who did not successfully convey their ideas in writing. Sometimes this may have been because they did not know how to do so; sometimes it may have been because they did not wish to expend the effort necessary to do so. We hope that students who fall into both of these categories will benefit from what we have to say.

This short book is intended to help students to develop essential intellectual and study skills in writing, reading and reasoning. Although written with students in mind we hope also that it will be of use to anyone who is concerned to develop such skills. It begins with a review of some differences between spoken and written forms of language. Later in the book we discuss a range of literary communication skills. For example, there are sections which focus on reading and writing, on rational argument, and on the importance of stylistic considerations in writing.

Our aims are threefold. First to facilitate the development of skill in successful writing through the use of a clear and effective style and an awareness of the requirements of cogent argument. Secondly, to help readers to develop skill in the reading and evaluation of analytic and descriptive texts, including the sympathetic, critical appraisal of arguments. Finally, to offer some guidance on basic study skills.

The book may be used in a number of ways. Some readers may choose to begin at the beginning and read the three parts in the order in which we have presented them. On the other hand, readers whose main concern is to find help in developing their skill as a writer may wish first of all to read Part 2 which is perhaps the most accessible section of the book and gives the most direct and basic advice. Others, who have an interest in the nature of argument and in developing their effectiveness in arguing for a point of view, may begin with Part 3. Others again may care to dip in at various points, or to select particular sections, especially in Part 2, which seem relevant to a particular problem. Since in Part 1 we discuss various ways of approaching a text and suggest that reading a book from cover to cover is not necessarily the most appropriate way of using study time, we will be delighted if readers use the book in any of these ways.

In the final stages of writing the book we began to be appalled at the likelihood that having offered advice to others about how to write we might then have ignored it ourselves. Then we realized that all we could do would be to confess to our readers that we are mere mortals, subject to the same weaknesses as everyone else. We therefore apologize for those places within these pages where you discover examples of things we have warned against. Since in the event of the book reaching the stage of a second edition, we would like to remove some of these mistakes, we will be extremely grateful to anyone who is willing to write to us pointing out stylistic infelicities or factual errors. We would be willing to pay a small amount of money to those helping us in this way: shall we say 50p per 'own goal'? (More than this amount we are afraid to offer for fear of the bankruptcy courts.)

It is common nowadays for writers to avoid the exclusive use of the masculine pronouns to indicate their awareness that there are 'shes' as well as 'hes' in the world. One way of doing this is to make sure that they use personal pronouns, for example 'she', 'he' or 'her' only when a specific person is being discussed and that, when they do so, they accurately match the pronouns used to the sex of the individual in question. Another possibility is to use the plural forms 'they', 'their' and 'them' in place of singular personal pronouns. We find the second of these two practices stylistically offensive. The first, in a book such as this, would be a difficult convention to adopt because we often use hypothetical examples. We have thought long and hard about this issue and have come up with the following convention. In all cases where the individual in question is a student, we have tried to use male pronouns. Where the individual is not identified as a student but is, for example, a lecturer or professional writer, we have tried to use female pronouns. This convention has been applied except in actual cases where to adopt it would be to mis-sex someone or where to stick with it would cause confusion. No doubt this convention will not satisfy everyone. For example, a dogged feminist might point out that it has resulted in more uses of the pronouns 'he', 'his' and 'him' than uses of their feminine counterparts (we have not counted). Or perhaps a chauvinistic man will point out that the convention we have adopted does not accurately portray the way things are in the real world where most lecturers are male rather than female. However, we have done our best.

There are a number of people we would like to thank for helping us with this book. Susan Fairbairn has discussed much of it with us and undertook a detailed reading of the final draft; Martin Stafford read the final draft and offered many valuable comments. We are grateful for their help. We are grateful also to Cathy Winch and Bob Solomon who offered helpful comments while we were working on the book.

Gavin Fairbairn
Chris Winch

# Part 1

Reading, Writing and Talking

# 1.1  Talking and writing

Talking is a more complicated business than many people realize. Being unaware of the full complexity of talk does not, of course, mean that you cannot communicate effectively. It may, however, prevent you from becoming a more effective communicator. More important, from our point of view, is that if you do not understand the complexities of speech you are unlikely to be aware of the very different techniques required when you are communicating through writing.

## Talking

Consider for a moment what goes into a conversational exchange between two or more people. Naturally, there are the words spoken, but the how, when and where of their being spoken is just as important in the sending of a message as the mere words. When we speak our tone of voice and facial expression convey attitude and emotion. Conversations take place in a particular situation and a certain amount of background knowledge common to speaker and listener is generally taken for granted. For example, a woman sitting in a café where an amusing incident happened before, might say to her friend, 'You remember the time when we . . .' and leave the rest of the sentence unsaid, but employ a grimace or a wry smile to evoke the incident in question for her listener. It might have been, for example, a time when they were both having a coffee and realized that neither of them had the money to pay the bill. A slight nod and smile from the listener is enough to show the woman that she has been understood. The physical situation of the café and the memory of shared experience are sufficient to convey her incompleted suggestion. Facial expression and gesture on the part of the listener reassure the speaker that her message has been understood.

What is left unsaid is often as important as what is said. For example, saying to a friend, 'Jimmy isn't drunk today' with a knowing look and in a certain tone of voice, could imply that he is drunk every other day. Even by simply changing the emphasis in the way in which one says something, one can quite change its meaning. One can even mean the *opposite* of what the words one is using mean when taken at face value. Someone who says, 'That's very kind of you' in the appropriate circumstances and with a shocked look, a bitter tone of voice and a stress on the first syllable of 'very', may well mean, 'That's very *unkind* of you'. The skilful listener will be aware of these possibilities, because the interpretation of nuances of meaning is something that we learn to do informally as we grow up and learn to speak and interact with others.

Possession of the appropriate background knowledge is also important in becoming an effective listener. I need to know the topic of conversation, that is, what is being talked about, and I need to know something about the topic in order to understand what I am being told. Even experienced listeners can find themselves lost in a conversation if they have entered it after it has started, or if they are not very knowledgeable about the topic. This problem can, to some extent, be remedied by asking questions and by making the most of the information one gets by listening very carefully to what is being said. The point is, however, that shared experience and knowledge are essential if we are to speak to each other effectively in most day-to-day contexts.

So talk takes place in a certain context. There is a speaker, a listener, and the social and physical situation that they are currently in. One of the most important features of talk is that there is the possibility of immediate interaction between speaker and listener. Among other things, this allows for missing information to be supplied on request in order that understanding can take place. If you don't understand what a person is saying, then at least if you are in face-to-face contact, you have the opportunity to ask for clarification.

All of us have had the opportunity to use the telephone, and we will have become aware (sometimes painfully) of the differences between speaking face to face and speaking over the telephone. The term 'face to face' alludes to these differences. Most people will also have heard the expression 'body language' used to describe the non-verbal aspects of face-to-face communication. Body language conveys much of the meaning that is conveyed in face-to-face talk; in telephonic talk it is absent. On the telephone, we do not see the other person's expressions. This means, for example, that though we may detect doubt in the listener's voice, we cannot see it in her face. If, in the course of a telephone conversation, someone makes a suggestion about which I am unhappy, I may reply, 'I suppose so . . .' in a hesitant tone. In face-to-face talk, on the other hand, you will see that I also have an unhappy facial expression as I am talking which makes my unease even clearer when taken together with my hesitant tone. It is also more difficult to detect insincerity over the telephone. We cannot see the uneasy facial expression on the speaker which might give the face-to-face listener cause to doubt the breezy confident tone in which for example the speaker says, 'Of course I can get it for you by tomorrow . . .'. Sometimes these features mean that speaking over the phone can have certain advantages. Consider, for example, how much easier it is to tell a lie over the phone; or think, for example, how much easier it would be to turn down an unwanted invitation over the telephone than face to face. On the other hand, telephonic communication can have disadvantages. Voices may sound unnatural, people may feel uneasy and pressed for time and the possibility of referring to objects physically in the environment of the speaker by a gesture or a demonstrative such as 'this cup' or 'that book' is not available.

*Exercise*
It might be helpful in trying to grasp what we are getting at here to spend some time thinking about the different requirements of passing on the same message in different ways. Imagine, for example, that you have to give a friend instructions on how to get to your new address. Think for a minute about how you might set about doing this over the telephone and how this might differ from what you would have to do if you were leaving the same message on his answering machine. Consider also whether it might be harder or easier to give these instructions face to face or in writing.

## How are talking and writing different?

Most of the differences between face-to-face talk and talk over the telephone also exist between face-to-face talk and written communication. For example, with writing as with telephonic talk, the physical context is not present to the reader and one cannot detect facial expression. On the other hand, there are some similarities between telephonic and face-to-face communication that are not shared with written communication. These include tone of voice and the possibility of interaction between speaker and listener. In both the speaker can take the listener 'for granted' in a sense, because she knows that he will be able to intervene to ask for more information or for clarification.

When you are writing to someone, tone of voice, physical proximity and the possibility of quick interaction are not available and you need to be able to communicate effectively without resorting to these features. Not having them available ought to make you aware of how important they are and should lead you to compensate accordingly when you write. However, our very familiarity with speech, the fact that we feel so much at ease with the spoken word and the fact that it 'comes naturally' to us, tend to make it all the more difficult to adjust to the different requirements of writing.

Because the clues which are supplied by context in spoken communication are not available to her readers, the writer has to make do without them and communicate effectively none the less. This involves substituting (if possible) for tone of voice, the physical presence of the listener, physical situation, and the possibility of interaction. For example, since you cannot look firm or sound firm in a letter you have to convey firmness in a different way, perhaps by using an expression such as 'I am absolutely determined that . . .'. And it is no good referring to an object in my room as 'the table over there', for example, if readers cannot see it. When communicating in a written form your readers cannot communicate directly with you and so when you use some such phrase as 'You remember the time when . . .' you will need to be sure that your reader really does remember such a time, because he may not understand what you are writing about if he does not, and the opportunity is not available to him to get you to jog his memory. Striking the right balance between what to leave out and what to put in is sometimes a fine judgement which depends on whom one is writing for. These matters will be dealt with at greater length in Part 2.

The points we have drawn attention to so far may all seem elementary aspects of making oneself understood in writing, but they constantly seem to get overlooked, particularly by people who do not write very often, or who are uneasy about writing. Even those who consider themselves accomplished writers and are well aware of these pitfalls, may ignore these features when the subject matter about which they are writing is abstract or unfamiliar. This is most likely to happen when the readership is assumed to be at least as knowledgeable as the writer about the subject matter. The writer may refer to a book, an argument or an individual which she assumes wrongly that the reader will know about. For example, she might refer casually to 'Zukowski's well-known recent monograph on the sexual habits of Outer Mongolian Lepidoptera', when in fact the reader has never heard of Zukowski or Outer Mongolian Lepidoptera, far less having any interest in their sexual habits. Unfortunately, there is no immediate way in which the reader can correct this impression. He has to make do with what is on the page in front of him.

# 1.2 What reading involves

The ability to read well is an art acquired, if we are lucky, when we are young. All of us, if we have reached the level of higher education, should be reasonably competent readers. It does not follow that we make the best possible use of this ability, or that we have developed it as much as we can. In this chapter advice will be given on making the best use of the time you have available for reading and on making yourself a better reader.

## Finding meaning in written texts

It may seem like an obvious thing to say, but we read in order to gain *meaning* from a text. It is technically possible to read and not to gain meaning in a language like ours. The *alphabetic* principle which governs our script and our spelling allows us to reproduce the sound of a sentence from print by following rules which convert print into sound. A very simple example such as

A dog sat on a log

can be spoken by saying the sound associated with each letter in a smooth sequence. Our spelling system is much more complicated and less regular than this simple example suggests of course. But the general alphabetic principle holds and, for example, allows us to sound out the above sentence without understanding a word of it.

### *Literal meaning*

Naturally we aim to read for meaning. Much of the meaning that we gain from what we read is *literal* in character; that is, words are used with their usual meanings. For example, in the sentence 'John went for a walk', all the words that compose the sentence are used in an everyday sense which everyone understands. Literal meaning is important and should be attended to. There are many kinds of writing in which it plays a crucial role in understanding, particularly where precision is required. Description, explanation, the giving of instructions, reportage and argumentation are all types of writing where literal meaning will, in many cases, play a vital role because in these areas it is important that there should be no misunderstanding on the part of the reader. It is, for example, necessary that a court report, a car assembly manual, an insurance claim, or a scientific hypothesis is not misunderstood through vagueness, the use of difficult metaphors or ambiguity; literal meaning will play a large role in these kinds of writing. Recipes, instructions, impersonal descriptions and explanations are all important and common examples of writing which employ literal meaning.

We do not always fully understand what we read, particularly when we do not understand the meanings of all the words employed in a sentence. In the sentence, 'John went for a walk', the meaning of the sentence is clear enough, provided that we know the meanings of the individual words which compose it. Meaning here is simply at the literal level. In other words if we know what the individual words mean and how they are put together in our language, we know what the sentence means.

Literal meaning is less important when the writer is trying to be witty or entertaining, where part of the effect of her writing may well depend on brevity, ambiguity, or the use of metaphor. As a reader you should attend carefully to literal meaning when the context and kind of writing involved suggest that this is important. If you are satisfied that a literal meaning is appropriate and you cannot find it, ask yourself whether this is due to a fault on your part or on the part of the author. In the first case it may be that there are some words whose meanings you do not understand. In the second case it may be that a word or phrase is ambiguous. You should either go to a dictionary and find out the literal meaning of the word in question, or you should note alternative meanings and select the one which seems most appropriate in the passage. It is important to be meticulous about this, as achieving a basic understanding of what an author is saying is essential in order to make a proper and fair assessment of it.

## *Metaphorical meaning*

So far we have been considering the importance of literal meaning, where an author communicates by using words in their everyday sense to convey meaning in a straightforward way. Consider by way of contrast the following:

Jill's toe injury left her a dead duck on the racetrack.

This is not a very elegant sentence but you will probably understand that it means that Jill had to withdraw from the race. You will not be inclined to think either that Jill was given a dead duck by her toe injury or that she was transformed into a dead duck by it. The expression 'dead duck' is not being used with its literal meaning here, but in what is called a metaphorical sense. Although when we read this sentence we do not believe for a moment that Jill has become a dead duck, we understand it readily enough because we know that in this context 'dead duck' means something like 'no longer able to function'. We know that this is the meaning of 'dead duck' in cases like this because the usage is not uncommon, both in writing and in everyday speech. You should never write something like:

> The university was literally caught with its trousers down.

A university could be caught with its trousers down in a metaphorical sense (that is, it could be caught in a state of embarrassing unpreparedness). But the sentence as it stands above is a piece of nonsense which shows with painful clarity the speaker's or writer's unwillingness or inability to acknowledge the distinction between literal and metaphorical meaning. The word 'literally' should not be used in contexts where a metaphor is intended. In the sentence:

> John's tutor literally blew his essay out of the water

literal meaning and metaphor are again confused, unless the writer means that John's essay was lying somewhere offshore and his tutor subjected it to an artillery barrage or that John's tutor had exceptionally strong lungs.

## Cultural literacy

In metaphorical uses of language the reader has to understand the metaphor or metaphors employed in order to understand the meanings the author is attempting to convey. In the next example meaning is conveyed in a straightforward, literal way, metaphor is not used, and yet many readers will not understand what the author means:

> Crofters were driven off the land in the clearances.

Though any reasonably competent reader of English prose will be able to read the above passage aloud, it does not necessarily follow that she will be able to understand it. Think for a moment about why this might be so.

Problems may be caused by a lack of clarity about the meanings of certain words, such as 'crofters' and 'clearances', in the sentence above. In addition, the reader needs to know more about what has gone before in the passage of text from which it comes and, generally speaking, what the passage is *about*. Inability to bring such information to bear will mean that the reader will not be able to grasp the *literal* meaning of the sentence. This information will consist in both general knowledge and also specialist knowledge of the area in which she is reading. In order to understand this sentence readers would have to know what crofters are and also some Scottish history. Crofters are tenants who farm small areas of land in the Scottish Highlands and Islands and 'clearances' in this sentence refers to a specific historical event that took place in the Highlands of Scotland rather than to department-store sales.

Both general knowledge and specialist knowledge about the area in which you are reading will help you to read with greater understanding. This is true both in the sense that by having such knowledge you will be helped to understand a wider range of vocabulary and in the sense that you will be helped to understand the specialized use of a word in a particular context. The term 'cultural literacy' is often used to describe the acquaintance with a common store of knowledge which any reasonably educated member of our society should have. Notice that this reference to culture does not necessarily imply a knowledge of what is sometimes referred to as 'high culture': opera, theatre, great literature and so on. It refers generally to the common store of knowledge about our society.

A broad general knowledge and a broad knowledge of your subject area will make you a more effective reader, so it is worth cultivating good reading habits such as reading widely, from the outset of your studies.

If you find that numerous dates, places, persons and events of which you are unaware are referred to in what you read you should try to do some general background reading in the main areas of human achievement including science, humanities and the arts. For example, it would be worthwhile reading a simple history of Europe and the UK, a compendium of science, and a simple but comprehensive geography text. Daily reading of a serious newspaper and the regular reading of both a popular science and current affairs weekly or monthly will also prove to be an invaluable aid to improving general reading ability by helping you to build up a store of background knowledge and associations with which to make sense of what you read. There is no single newspaper or journal that we would wish to recommend, but among the daily newspapers, the reader has a choice of at least four papers which give a fairly thorough presentation and analysis of current news in a fairly impartial way (the views of the editorials, of course, are very different): *The Times*, the *Daily Telegraph*, the *Independent* and the *Guardian*. Among the weeklies, *The Economist* and the *London Review of Books* would be valuable. Watching and listening to current affairs programmes and programmes about scientific, geographical, historical and aesthetic topics on the radio and television can also be invaluable in building up this background cultural knowledge.

## Metaphors that depend on cultural literacy

Sometimes writers mix metaphor and cultural literacy in order to express complex ideas in a short form. In order to understand such uses of language a reader will need both to understand the cultural references on which it depends and also that the sentence or phrase is employing language in a metaphorical rather than a literal way. For example, the sentence

Jones was the Bill Haley of the retailing revolution

only makes sense if the reader has some notion of who Bill Haley was, what he did and what happened to him, and if they can see how the idea of a revolution can be applied to an activity such as retailing. A very basic knowledge of the changes that occurred in popular music in the 1950s would tell a reader that Bill Haley was one of the more important and innovative figures in popular music at that time, but who was eventually succeeded by other figures who became more influential and more fashionable than him. If we suppose that 'retailing revolution' refers to the practice of building out-of-town hypermarkets which sell just about everything, it can be fairly safely inferred that the sentence is about a retailer who set about selling through out-of-town hypermarkets with such vigour that he put a lot of his rivals in the retail trade out of business but eventually lost touch himself and lost ground to younger rivals with a greater sense of what the public wanted at the time.

The sentence 'Jones was the Bill Haley of the retailing revolution' used common cultural knowledge to express a series of ideas in a very concise and metaphorical way. A problem with the use of such cultural references is that the reader needs to have the necessary background knowledge before she can make the associations that alone give sense to such a statement. This kind of association is very common in most fields, from newspapers to specialist publications, and the reader is seriously handicapped if she does not have sufficient cultural literacy to understand associations that a reasonably knowledgeable person should be able to grasp without any difficulty.

## Literal, inferential and evaluative comprehension of texts

We now turn to a consideration of the different levels at which texts can be understood.

Understanding the literal meaning of a passage is an important prerequisite to deeper understanding, but is not the end of the business of considering and using what a text has to offer. In order to make use of what you have read, it will be necessary to make sure that you can recall the most important points in the passage including, for example, the development of an argument. This will probably mean that you have to re-read the passage or take notes before recalling it in your own words. Almost certainly you will not wish to recover everything that you have read, but only the most important points for your own particular purpose. When you read a text for the first time you should keep in mind what is important to you in reading it.

### *Reorganizing*

Very often it will be necessary for you to read more than one article or book in order to find what you need. The information you require may come from more than one source and you will need to put it together in a way that suits your purpose. It may also be necessary to ignore some information which is not strictly relevant to what you are after. In these cases it will be necessary for you to *reorganize* what you have read into a suitable form, and the note-taking and purposeful attitude to reading which are required for recall will also be necessary for successful reorganization. Reorganization then will be a particularly useful technique when you are relying on more than one source for your information. It will involve selecting what is important in each of the sources and putting together what you have learned in a way that is coherent and relevant to your own particular concerns. You should not attempt this until you are confident about recalling what is important to you from a single passage.

## *Inferring*

An experienced reader should be able to *infer* meaning beyond what is literally stated on the page. This process of inference covers a wide variety of cases. If you were to read in a newspaper that 'the spokesman declined to comment further on the matter' when he was speaking about a sensitive issue, you would probably conclude that there was a great deal more to say, but that it was of such a sensitive nature that the spokesman did not wish to reveal any more. You would probably be correct in your inference, but not necessarily; it is possible that the spokesman had a sore throat and lost his voice, for example.

Again, if you were to read in a review of a restaurant that none of the diners became ill after the meal, you would not take this as a compliment to the chef or the proprietor, but would infer that it was by luck that no one became ill and that the restaurant was really awful. The reason for this, of course, is that it is unusual to mention the health of the diners in a restaurant review. By going out of her way to draw the reader's attention to the health of the diners, the reviewer has aroused the reader's suspicions. He will ask, 'Why should this matter be mentioned?' and will search around for possible reasons. It could be, of course, that the reviewer was obsessed with hygiene and made this comment with perfectly straightforward intentions. If she were sued for libel by the restaurateur, she could perfectly well claim that she had not literally accused the restaurant of being unhygienic.

Suppose that you were to read the following sentence in a report on a sociological survey:

The hypothesis was not rejected at the 0.1 level of significance.

This will seem straightforward enough to the reader with some basic knowledge of the use of statistics in the social sciences who would understand from this statement that there was less than a 1 in 10 chance that the results of the survey arose randomly. However, someone more knowledgeable about statistics would want to ask why the significance level was set so low rather than at, say 0.01 or even 0.001 as would be more normal in social research (these would imply respectively that there was less than a 1 in 100 or 1 in 1000 chance of the results occurring randomly). He might well infer that the hypothesis would have been rejected if a higher significance level had been chosen and that therefore the author of the report must have some reason for wishing to conceal this fact.

There are other cases where you can safely infer something from what you have read without room for doubt. If you read that all whales breathe air and that Freddie is a whale, you may deduce that Freddie breathes air, even though this is not stated on the page. This is an example of a deductive argument. The nature of deductive argument is discussed in some detail in Part 3 where it is also distinguished from inductive argument.

For the moment you should be aware of the possibility of reading into a text more than is actually there. As a reader you should be alert to the possibility that there is more to what an author wishes to communicate to you than she actually states on the page. However, you should also be aware of the limitations of this technique. You do not want to read into a passage more than you are entitled to and therefore you very often need to draw conclusions from inferential comprehension in a tentative way.

## Evaluating

Another aspect of going beyond literal meaning is that you will be *evaluating* what you are reading; that is, you will be forming an opinion as to the worth of what you are reading. Does the author present good arguments or evidence for her assertions? Is information easy to find? Does the author express views which are consistent with one another? Does she distinguish clearly between what is fact and what is opinion, or does opinion often masquerade as fact? In order to be able to arrive at judgements of this kind, you will need to be able to make inferences from what you read. If you are comparing two texts covering the same ground you may well wish to compare their treatment; here an ability to recall what is written will be necessary before you evaluate. The point is that there is much more to effectively reading a text than understanding and being able to recall literally what it means, but if you are unable to do this effectively you will not be able to undertake the interpretative activities of reorganization, inference and evaluation.

An important point both for recall and for evaluation is that you should attempt to make a sympathetic appraisal of what you are reading. In the case of recall, if there are omissions or ambiguities in what you read, you will need to consider what further facts can be safely assumed or inferred before the text makes perfectly clear sense. When you are reading a passage, you will need to be sure that you have properly understood what the author was trying to say before you evaluate or criticize it, even if she is being obscure or ambiguous. If you fail to do this, you may well have fun making a destructive evaluation or criticism of the author, but at the expense of missing the point of what she is trying to say.

## Reading in different ways

Reading systematically for understanding demands patience and is time-consuming. However, it is possible to take short cuts to locate passages that will repay reading in a systematic way. Using such short cuts will help you to develop effective ways of using your reading time. What you need are ways of locating text that you wish to read systematically and what follows are some suggestions for doing this which you should practise and use, almost as second nature.

(i)    Use the organizational features of the text you are reading to see whether it is really what you want or to find the passage that is of particular interest to you. The *title* should provide some indication of whether or not the book or article is in your general field of interest. In the case of a book you should also consult the information given on the *jacket or flyleaf*, in the table of *contents* and the *index*.

The contents page of a book will give you some idea of what it is about. However, it may not tell you in enough detail for you to be able to identify the particular area of interest that you need to know about; the index should provide a more detailed list of topics and people covered and their exact location. It is always advisable, therefore, to use the index as a means of locating what you are looking for, or for seeing if a book contains relevant information. *Bibliographies* or *reference lists* located at the end of each chapter or of the text as a whole, and the *preface* or *introduction* will also give a general indication of whether the book is worth reading more closely. Time taken in flicking through the book looking briefly at, for example, the beginnings and ends of chapters and sections will be worthwhile.

In the case of articles there are also organizational features which it is worth learning to use. Some articles have an *abstract* or brief account of the contents which should tell you if it is worth proceeding further. Even if the article does not have an abstract at the beginning, it is worth reading the first paragraph in order to get some indication of whether the title lives up to its promise of the article being something worth reading. Some journals have a list of keywords at the beginning, which allows the reader to assess whether or not the article is in her field of interest. Articles will have a bibliography or footnotes. A quick glance at these will tell you whether or not the article falls within your range of interest.

References in a bibliography may be organized according to the 'author-date system' sometimes known as the 'Harvard system', which we discuss in Part 2. A second method of referencing, using footnotes, is found in some journals. In this system, which is also discussed in Part 2, numbered footnotes are referred to by numbers in the text. A disadvantage of this system is that the reader has to turn to the notes to see information which in the Harvard system would be displayed in the text. However, it does allow you to intersperse genuine notes or comments together with the references. The references are very easy to find as they are organized in numerical order, and often have cross-references between different footnotes. In the following example the author refers both to some work by Atkinson and to work by Bernstein that Atkinson discusses:

> I hope to show that Atkinson's (1) interpretation of Bernstein as not being interested in a developmental model cannot be sustained by any detailed reference to the textual evidence (2).

A reader who wishes to refer to the views that the author is criticizing will find details about where to find Atkinson's work under footnote 1; one who wishes to have a look at the work of Bernstein that Atkinson discusses will find details under footnote 2.

(ii) If you think that you have located a relevant chapter, article or passage, and the procedures outlined in (i) above have not been enough to tell you exactly where the topic that you want is located, or whether it is included at all, you should try *skimming* through the text. This will involve reading it very quickly in order to get the general drift or a sense of what is covered. There is no special technique for skimming: the reader tries to take in as much of the text as possible, working down the page as well as across, sometimes *skipping* or leaving out chunks of text that do not seem to be relevant or which can be anticipated with ease. If you come to a word, phrase or sentence that you think is relevant to your concerns, then you may slow down and read that passage more closely. Another technique is to read, at a normal pace, the first and last paragraphs of a chapter, followed by the first and last sentences of each paragraph, thus building up a sketchy overall picture of the contents of a passage, shifting to systematic reading when it seems relevant (this is a technique sometimes known as *sampling*). Sampling and skimming can be fruitfully used together. When they are, the technique is sometimes known as *previewing*. None of these is really a rapid reading technique: rather, each is a way of gaining an overall sense of the text as a preliminary to determining whether or not it requires closer attention. If you want to learn more about reading fast, you may care to consult De Leeuw and De Leeuw's popular book, *Read Better, Read Faster* (1963).

If you have found a specific index heading of a particular word or phrase that you wish to locate, then you will need rapidly to *scan* the relevant passage until you locate the word or phrase. Here you do not need to read carefully or even to get the general drift of a passage, but you should just be able to recognize what you are looking for when you happen to come across it. A related technique here is that of *search reading* where you read rapidly, not looking for a particular word or phrase but just searching for words or phrases that are relevant to your topic (Beard 1987). This technique, in contrast to skimming, is useful when you are interested in finding out not so much the general drift, but rather whether or not the chapter or article addresses your particular area of concern.

You should become used to 'changing gear' in your reading: skimming and scanning until you locate the particular area of interest then switching to a normal reading speed. On occasions you will need to read and re-read a passage until you are satisfied that you understand it and all its implications. This is sometimes known as *intensive reading*.

(iii)  Your reading can be made more purposeful by having specific questions in mind. These may be questions that you are already bringing to the text or they may be questions suggested by the procedures described in (i) and (ii) above. When you have skimmed an article or looked through the contents page of a book and gained some idea of what is contained in it you can read the book or parts of the book or the article with specific questions in mind. When you have read the text you can then ask yourself whether or not your questions have been answered, recite the answers to yourself mentally or in note form, and finally ask yourself whether or not what you have learned satisfies the questions that you have formulated or whether you need to formulate new questions in order to pursue your topic of interest. If you have failed to get a question answered, is this because of faults in your own questioning strategy or because the material you are reading is organized badly? You may even need to consider whether some information which might reasonably be expected to be in a text of that type has been inexplicably omitted.

## SQ3R

We have been discussing ways of making your reading more effective by the use of some informal changes to your reading style. The technique of *SQ3R* or *Survey, Question, Read, Recite, Review* (Beard 1987) can be a useful way of approaching a text in a systematic and enquiring manner. As you grow more experienced, it is a technique that you may come to use without thinking. When you are starting to use it, however, it is helpful to do so with a partner or even in a group so that you gain more confidence by having other points of view to set against your own.

Let us consider how a reader might apply SQ3R to a variety of reading tasks at different levels of complexity.

(i)   The first example is simple and based on a book for older children, *Aborigines* by Virginia Luling (1982). This may seem to be much too easy an exercise for anyone in higher education, but we have found that many college students have had difficulty with it.

Imagine that you have been asked to use the book *Aborigines* to find out about Aborigine marriage customs and, more precisely, exactly who can marry whom.

A quick *survey* of the book will not reveal anything obvious. Looking at the table of contents will not reveal any explicit reference to marriage, but on p. 28 there is a chapter on childhood and on p. 30 a chapter about later life. Since you are likely to get married after childhood, you might infer that the chapter on later life seems promising. If you were to turn to it you would find that there is indeed quite a lot of information about Aborigine marriage, but nothing that answers the question you have been set. Since none of the other content headings seem to be any more promising, you might need to ask yourself 'Where else might I find the information that I want?' You will now be in the *question* phase of the exercise. The other major information-seeking section of the book that is likely to tell you where the information that you want is located, is the index. The contents will tell you that the index is found on p. 48 and the index will tell you that marriage is referred to on pp. 22, 23 and 30. On p. 30 you will find the chapter entitled 'Later life', to which you have already referred. However, on p. 22 you will find a chapter entitled 'An Ordered World', which explains the clan and moiety system in Aborigine society in some detail. This chapter will give you the information that you want, namely which people are allowed to marry each other. This is the section that you will need to *read* in detail and make notes on.

After this stage you will wish to *recite* what you have learned, to check that you have really answered your question. Finally you can *review* the whole process, including the difficulties of locating the information that you wanted. It may seem to be a reasonable complaint that the chapter on 'An Ordered World' had not been entitled something like 'Marriage Customs'. On the other hand, you cannot reasonably expect the author's priorities in the organizing of her book to coincide exactly with your own. Virgina Luling was not just concerned with marriage, but with broader issues about how Aborigine society is organized and to entitle the chapter 'Marriage' or something like that would not have captured her intentions properly. You might well realize in your review stage just how valuable a good index can be, since it reflects far more accurately the range of concerns addressed in a book than the table of contents, which, quite rightly, reflects the author's organizational priorities.

In discussing this imaginary exercise we have gone through the five stages in SQ3R. Let us now present them to you in a form that is easy to refer to.

*Summary of stages in SQ3R*

| | |
|---|---|
| *Survey* | What is the text about? |
| *Question* | What do I want to know? <br> Where in the text can I find it? |
| *Read* | Does the text contain the information I need? |
| *Recite* | What have I learned? |
| *Review* | Have I found what I wanted? <br> What are the next steps? <br> What further texts should I look at? |

(ii)   Next let us look at a more complex example based on a book for adults, *Madhur Jaffrey's Indian Cookery* (Jaffrey 1982). Suppose that you have been asked to use this book to find out some information about the dish called *saag aloo*: the English translation for the Indian name, the ingredients and which meat, chicken or fish dishes it is suitable to accompany. First of all, you will have to *survey* the book and gain a general idea of what it is about and how it is organized. You may notice on the contents page that there are chapters with broad subject headings such as 'Meat', 'Fish' and 'Vegetables'. Turning to look at individual chapters you will find recipes. Each recipe is headed by the English name of the dish with the Indian name underneath. There is a short introduction to each dish which usually indicates what other dish can suitably accompany it. Underneath, the page is divided into two sections. On the left in bold print is a list of ingredients. On the right are the instructions for cooking the dish.

You will now write down what you wish to find out and formulate some idea of the order in which you want to look for the answers to your *questions*. Having completed the question phase, you will now begin the *read* phase of your enquiry. From your survey of the book you will know that the chapter headings are too broad in subject matter to help you to locate *saag aloo* directly, so you will probably look in the index. This indicates that the dish is located on p. 116. Turning to this page you will notice immediately that the English name of the the dish, spinach with potatoes, is at the top of the page. The introduction to the recipe will tell you that *saag aloo* is a suitable accompaniment for *rogan josh*, or red lamb or beef stew. You will also note that the recipe for this is on p. 51. You can copy down the ingredients on the left-hand side of the page. You will not be able to find a further reference to *saag aloo* in the index so you will finish the *read* phase at this stage.

When you *recite* what you have learned, you will realize that you have obtained all the information that you wanted except for the names of any other dishes that *saag aloo* might suitably accompany. Finally, when you come to review the enquiry, you may wonder whether or not there might be another way of locating any dishes which *saag aloo* can accompany. At this point you may recall noticing that although *rogan josh* is mentioned on p. 116 the index does not list it as being on that page. This will raise the possibility that not every occurrence of a dish is listed in the index. Perhaps only the most important references are listed there. You will now go back to the *read* phase and look systematically through the introductions to the recipes in the meat, chicken and fish chapters. On p. 94 you will notice that it is mentioned as an accompaniment for haddock baked in a yoghurt sauce, even though there is not an entry for *saag aloo* on this page in the index.

By now you will have discovered all the information you require and you will return to the *review* phase and note for future reference that sometimes it is necessary to work through a text page by page, scanning or search-reading in order to find what you want. When authors are constructing indexes they will make decisions about which entries they want to include and whether to put in all the page references or only the major ones. Once again, you may note that the author's priorities might not be the same as yours and that you need to take account of this in your reading.

(iii) Finally let us turn to a more difficult example of the technique, one which brings out more clearly the importance of both general and specific background knowledge in successful reading for information. Let us suppose that you have been asked to write a long assignment on the educational effects of streaming primary school pupils; 'streaming' refers to the educational practice of grouping children according to their stage of learning or, more bluntly, according to ability. You have material which reports research done in the 1960s and early 1970s but you might wish to find out what more up-to-date research can tell you about the effects of streaming. One natural place to look would be in recent research on what makes primary schooling effective. After researching in the library for some time you might come across *School Matters*, a report of research on the determinants of effective junior schooling carried out in the Inner London Education Authority (Mortimore *et al.* 1988) which looks as if it should be worth investigating. The table of contents does not mention streaming as such but contains a number of headings which look as if they might be promising. *This is the survey stage of your enquiry.* For example, a glance at the title of Chapter 2: 'The Schools', might suggest that it may well contain information about streamed and unstreamed schools. You will now read this section with a specific question in mind, probably something like: 'What can this chapter tell me about the effects of streaming on educational achievement?' *This is the question stage.*

Chapter 2 is very systematically divided into three sets of subsections. Under 'School Policies' you will find a further subheading,

'Criteria for allocation to class'. Scanning this subsection for 'stream-ing' or 'ability grouping' will tell you nothing that you particularly wish to know, until you come to the heading 'Other criteria for the allocation of pupils to classes', which refers to allocation on the basis of criteria other than age. By systematically reading this section you will see that 'Approximately nine per cent of heads grouped children according to their stage of learning' (op. cit. p. 15). You will also learn that most schools group single-age classes on the basis of a mix of different abilities. *This is the read stage.*

What you have learned so far is at least consistent with the possibility that some schools in the survey may stream according to ability. One problem is that the authors do not appear to use the term 'streaming' in connection with ability grouping, so you will not be able to tell whether or not this book is going to address your concerns exactly.

It may at this stage be helpful to turn to the index to see if there is any reference to what you are looking for. There is not an entry for 'streaming'; under 'ability' there are no subheadings related to streaming. However, your own reading in the area may have included one of the key studies of streaming published in the 1970s, namely Barker-Lunn (1970) and, on turning to the bibliography, you will find that it is cited there. If you turn again to the index looking for references to Barker-Lunn you will find several. However, following up these references will not produce any direct comment on the research on streaming and achievement.

By this stage you will have employed a variety of different techniques of reading: organizational searching of contents, bibli-ographies, indexes and chapter subheadings; skimming; scanning for the word 'streaming'; search reading for relevant words, phrases or headings, and careful, systematic reading of the subsection on 'Other criteria for the allocation of pupils to classes'.

You will now be in a position to *recite* what you have gained in knowledge about streaming from looking at this book. The answer will probably be: 'Very little'. There is some reference to the literature on streaming, an oblique reference to the fact that some heads may stream their pupils (grouping according to stage of learning), and that is all. On going to the *review* stage of your enquiry you will ask yourself just what you have found out from your reading. On the surface, very little. Certainly, the *literal* meaning of the text of Mortimore's book will give you very little. Even the reference to grouping 'according to stages of learning' cannot entitle you to *infer* that these heads actually practised streaming. For example, it may just be that the schools in Mortimore's survey have pupils from different backgrounds or from different schooling systems and may wish to take account of this in their grouping, perhaps on a temporary basis. Nevertheless, there is a likelihood that the practice of streaming is included under this heading.

It is quite likely that you will end your reading of Mortimore on something of a note of disappointment, since you have neither gained any direct new information nor located any promising new references. However, if you are very determined you could carry the review process further. In doing so, you will need to bring into play what you already know. You will know from your reading about this subject that since the abolition of the eleven-plus, streaming in primary schools has become rarer but not non-existent. You will also know that it could be a sensitive issue in educational politics. Several of the fifty schools in the survey may have practised streaming and data concerning achievement would have been gathered from them. These considerations might lead you to wonder whether or not the researchers *had* in fact derived conclusions based on the relationship between streaming and achievement and whether the information thus obtained was omitted through accident or design. At this stage you will be *evaluating* what you have read. For example, does the book give a complete picture of the factors relevant to effective junior schooling? Would it have given a more satisfactory picture if it had at least made some specific reference to streaming? As a result of these reflections you may even wish to write to one of the authors to seek further information on the issues that interest you.

We have now discussed the various stages of SQ3R and illustrated them by references to three examples. You should now try using this technique in connection with a book that you are reading or an assignment that you are currently writing. Once you have used this technique several times you will find that you are able to go through it informally without having to consciously remind yourself of each stage.

## Taking notes

This seems to be an appropriate place to make some remarks on note-taking since it is an essential aspect of the different forms of understanding text that we discussed earlier. There are many different ways of taking notes and you have to find a system that works for you. However, here are a few points about one possible approach that you might like to try.

(i)   Do not make notes on the text, but in a separate notebook or set of cards. It does not do to deface books, including your own, as they are spoiled for future use. A textbook is also a very cumbersome place in which to store notes. If you need to mark a passage for note-taking, do so with a cross in the margin in light pencil which you can recognize and then rub out immediately after use. Above all, don't deface a book with your outraged immediate reactions to what you have read. Your reactions are important but they can wait for calmer reflection before you set them down on paper.

(ii)   Keep your notes in an accessible place. A large, lined, exercise book is suitable for this purpose and it is advisable to make a table of contents of the different books and articles on which you have made notes in the covers of the exercise book for easy reference.

(iii)  Once you have located a passage which you think will be of use to you, read it first and then take notes. You need to develop a feel for what is essential and what is not, and therefore you need to get the general structure of the argument or the exposition of information before you can decide what to take down and what to leave. These decisions will also depend on what you already know and have already read and you will sometimes want just to cross-reference with another text rather than make extensive notes on this particular one.

(iv)   Make notes in your own words; they do not have to be fully articulated sentences, but they must be clear enough for you to be able to read them when you come back to them. It is important that you do this, because it is a way of coming to grips with the text, seeing what is essential and expressing that in your own words. This is essential for recall and reorganization of the material.

(v)    Suggesting that you should make notes using your own words does not mean that you should not transcribe direct quotations from the text, but you should keep these fairly rare. Only where you feel that a quotation is particularly apt or where it expresses an idea so clearly that you could not put it better yourself, even in note form, should you quote verbatim. You need not confine yourself to recall and reorganization, but should include cross-references to other texts where you think that this is appropriate, inferences that you think can be made or are intended by the author to be made and evaluative comments about the text from your own point of view. Do not confine these last to exclamations and expletives, but try to give reasons for your reactions. It is good that you react strongly to what you are reading, it is a sign that you are making an effort to get to grips with the subject and that the text is engaging your interest. You need to harness these reactions in such a way that they are going to be of use to you and therefore they need to be put in a form that you can use later.

(vi)   Be ready to learn from the writing of others how to improve (or in some cases, how not to improve), your own writing. Make notes of what you think are particularly good examples of style, in terms of sentence structure, vocabulary or metaphor so that you can make use of them yourself in your own writing. If you see clumsy style, pompous vocabulary or mixed metaphors, you can make a note of these in order to avoid using them yourself in the future.

# 1.3 What writing involves

In Section 1.2 we discussed the nature of reading: what is involved in making sense of written and printed material. We discussed the importance for students of being able to read effectively in a number of different ways. In this section we will have a look at what is involved in writing: at what is involved in committing ideas to paper or to computer disc. Although we will focus on a particular form of writing, involving the presentation of ideas and arguments, some features are common to all, including poetry, narrative fiction, advertising copy, scientific report writing, and the presentation of legal agreements using the technical jargon of the law.

Writing, like speaking, is a form of communication. In any form of writing, the writer normally has someone other than herself to whom she intends to communicate though in some circumstances, for example, when writing notes in a lecture or in keeping a personal diary, one addresses oneself as audience. Some forms of writing aim at presenting facts and some at presenting arguments in order to support conclusions, while others are about conveying feelings and impressions. But all are about communication.

*Exercise*
What do the following forms of writing aim at communicating and what differences in style, layout and so on might you expect to find in each?

a poem
a scientific report
a legal contract
an essay on the subject you are studying
a field guide to British birds
a novel
details from an estate agent about a house for sale
a letter to a friend
a leading article in a serious newspaper
a major article in a tabloid newspaper
a letter of application for a job.

Writing is about conveying meaning by selecting words and putting them together in a written or printed form. When you write you will most often be concerned that those who read your work will understand what you intend to say in a fairly simple way. At times, however, you may want to be more ambitious than this and provoke your reader into thinking creatively about something or into seeing the world differently than she has before. For students this can be a dangerous enterprise although it is enjoyable for lecturers when it is successful.

Professional writers are more free to write in a provocative manner because they have less to prove than students and in addition they are likely to be more sure of their ability to succeed. For example, in a rather contentious paper in applied philosophy, John Harris (1975) proposed a lottery in which the names of everyone would be entered; in the event of a shortage of organs for 'spare-part' surgery the person whose name was randomly selected from the list would be sacrificed to allow the needy individual to be saved. It is doubtful whether Harris ever intended this article to be taken seriously. What is not in doubt, however, is that 'The Survival Lottery' provoked a large number of people into thinking not only about the distinction between killing and letting die, but also about resource allocation in medicine.

In Section 1.1 we discussed some important limitations of writing. However, it is important to realize that writing has positive, enabling qualities as well. For example, one can supplement the text that one is writing with pictures, diagrams and maps. This would mean for instance that it might have been easier to send your friend a map showing her how to get to your house rather than to tell her via her answering machine.

Because writing is frequently used to communicate over distance and time, it exists in a fairly permanent form and it can be physically transported to the reader. The development of writing enabled mankind to cope efficiently with the need for communication over long distances before the advent of electronic media.

The permanence of print or writing gives it another important quality, that of *surveyability*. Unless it is recorded and can be played back and analysed, a spoken message is lost once delivered. This is not the case with writing; a written message can be re-read and examined closely and the text may be searched for ambiguity, unclarity or hidden meaning by 'reading between the lines'. In this way, an apparently passive reader can be quite a searching and active one. This is particularly likely to be the case in circumstances where the text is to be assessed in some way as, for example, in an academic context where an essay, project, book or article is being evaluated. In another way, of course, the reader is passive in relation to the author; she cannot respond immediately to him; there is no possibility of a quick reaction. Finally, the reader tends to be a much more remote figure for the writer than she does for the speaker. This is true even when the reader is, for example, an old friend to whom you are writing a letter. However, when the reader is known only slightly or even not at all, she is likely to be even more remote. This makes it hard for the inexperienced writer to keep a proper idea in mind of the person for whom he is writing and hard to write specifically to that person.

## Three important points about writing as a student

Three points therefore need to be borne in mind when one is planning a piece of writing, particularly if it is to be an important one such as an article or an essay.

(i)   Your text can be re-read and analysed over and over again. On each occasion different aspects and interpretations may occur to the reader.

(ii)  Your reader will be able to formulate ideas in her own mind about what you are saying or meaning but will usually not be able to ask you any questions at the time of reading. You will need to ask yourself the questions your reader might be inclined to ask in order to save her the fruitless task of asking and not being able to get an answer.

(iii) Do not be afraid of patronizing your readers by supplying infor-mation, references or arguments that you think are 'obvious' because they may not be obvious. For example, the writer who referred in an offhand way to Zukowski's work on Lepidoptera made the mistake of assuming that her readers shared her own peculiar enthusiasms. Your reader may be familiar with the subject matter about which you are writing and as a student your writing will often be in part an illustration of your own knowledge or grasp of a topic. However, even in such circumstances your readers will be interested in seeing whether or not you do in fact have that particular knowledge or grasp. You must, therefore, carefully weigh up the requirements of the particular person for whom you are writing, bearing in mind that she will not be able to question you about what you have written, although she will be able to study it carefully.

In Part 1 we have discussed some of the important differences between spoken and written language and the freedoms and constraints involved in each. In Part 2 we will offer some practical recommendations for writing that can be drawn from reflecting on the needs of a readership, relating, for example, to the need for clarity and the importance of ensuring that one's position is coherent.

# Part 2

Writing as a Student

# 2.1 Introduction

Later in Part 2 we will discuss such important matters as style and clarity. In the third part we will discuss the presentation of cogent arguments. Meantime, however, we want to draw attention to some more basic aspects of writing to which you should attend whenever you write. For example, you should attend as closely as possible to the spelling of words; a student who presents work which is poorly spelled will at best be thought uneducated and at worst lazy. You must try to write legibly; a student whose writing is poor is likely to be thought lazy and inconsiderate. It is irritating to read essays by students who seem to think one has little else to do than guess at what word is intended by a scrawl. If your handwriting is poor try to buy or borrow a typewriter or word processor. Alternatively you may care to invest some money that might have been spent on other things in paying to have your work typed for you.

## Guess what she's thinking

Sometimes students think that essay writing involves doing little more than persuading someone else that they are in possession of certain ideas, knowledge or facts. This may be called the 'Guess what she's thinking' attitude to essays and exams because it usually arises when the student has the misguided impression that a correct answer is lodged somewhere in the mind of the lecturer and all he has to do is to guess what she's thinking. Sometimes, of course, demonstrating that one possesses particular knowledge is a large part of the task involved in giving an adequate answer to a question. However, this is not always the case and if in doubt you should always make sure that you understand what is required by checking with the person who set the question or task.

Even when you are expected to demonstrate knowledge, you should beware of simply regurgitating notes you have taken in lectures. This mistake is not uncommon, particularly in answers written in examinations. You should also beware of the possibility of plagiarizing ideas drawn from books and articles you have read or have come across through other means, including for example, radio and television programmes and personal conversations. By 'plagiarizing' is meant using ideas that derive from others as if they are your own. This is particularly bad when you also use their words. Always refer to authors you have read or people with whom you have spoken and whom you recognize to have had an influence on your work. Of course it will be difficult to be aware of everything that has influenced your ideas. However, at the least you should avoid using other people's words and thoughts as if they are your own. At times you will find (as most of us do) that a bright idea you have hit upon has already been advanced by an important thinker many years or, perhaps in the case of a discipline like philosophy, many *hundreds* of years earlier. This is frustrating; but how nice to discover that you have been thinking along the same lines as an important writer from the past. In such a case we suggest that you refer to the fact that the ideas you have had have already been explored by others without attributing your ideas to them; this shows that you have made the attempt to work out how your ideas fit into the grand scheme of human intellectual endeavour while enabling you to own such ideas as your own creation.

# 2.2  Different kinds of student writing

Although in this book we tend to refer to 'essays' when discussing student writing, we recognize that not all written tasks a student is expected to carry out will take this form. Nevertheless, for the sake of simplicity, we will sometimes use the word 'essay' in a generic way to refer to any piece of writing required of students as part of their course. Though for convenience we often refer to all essays as if they are written as answers to questions, we recognize that often essays are written in response to an instruction rather than a question, for example, 'Compare the traditional music of Scotland with that of Ireland'.

Clearly there will be different expectations of students working within different areas of academic study. For example, the requirements of a project report in a science or social science discipline might include a formal review of relevant literature, the use of tables and diagrams, and the presentation of statistical analyses of data along with a discussion of the implications of these. On the other hand an essay in history or philosophy might be expected to focus on the presentation of coherent arguments in favour of a conclusion with reference being made to other literature only where this serves to support the conclusion being put forward.

Differences exist not only between the expectations of different disciplines but also between different kinds of student writing. What is expected of a student in writing a one-hour answer in an examination will be different from what will be expected when he is writing a 2,000-word essay or a 20,000-word dissertation on the same topic. Although in each case the examiner might reasonably expect that the student would have made a coherent attempt to cover the subject matter, different levels of detail in terms of argument, background knowledge and so on would be expected in each case. For example, in an exam answer, it would not normally be expected that detailed references would be given to other literature. However, this would be required in essays, dissertations and theses. And whereas there can be some excuse in an exam answer for a failure to give a coherent structure to an answer, this can hardly be excused in either of the other cases. One way in which longer and shorter pieces of writing are identical is the need in each case to ensure that you do not squander the words available to you. Too often students regard longer word limits as an excuse for rambling on and for relaxing the need to make every word and every sentence count for something.

## Different types of essay

The purposes of essays vary. Some are intended to give students the opportunity to demonstrate how much they have learned about an area of study. Others are intended to find out how well they can think about a particular conceptual or practical problem. All offer the student the opportunity to show that he has read work relating to the topic and more importantly that he can think, and has thought, about it.

Let us now say a little about the different kinds of essay that a student may be required to write; here we are using 'essay' in its more limited sense.

Not all essays ask questions. Some ask for description or comparison of, for example, two or more events, persons, sets of ideas or states of affairs. Others ask for discussion or evaluation. There are different ways in which essays may be grouped according to what they expect of students. One possible way of doing this is to categorize them as involving description, discussion, evaluation or comparison. Let us give some examples of each of these:

*Description*
(i)   Write an account of the causes of the Second World War.
(ii)  Describe Darwin's theory of evolution.
(iii) Describe the use of behaviourist psychology in schools.

*Discussion*
(i)   Discuss the causes of the Second World War.
(ii)  Discuss the view that Darwin's evolutionary theory brought about a revolution in nineteenth-century thought.

(iii) Discuss the influence that behaviourist psychology has had on schools.

*Evaluation*
(i)   Critically evaluate Mead's account of the causes of the Second World War.
(ii)  Does Darwin's theory of evolution allow us to explain how the flora and fauna of the earth have attained their present forms?
(iii) How successful is behaviourist psychology in explaining human behaviour and experience?

Essays that ask for description, discussion and evaluation lay different expectations on the student. They may be thought of as requiring different levels of commitment or involvement from students.

Descriptive essays require the student simply to describe something, for example, an event, state of affairs, theory or practice. Though descriptive essays are probably the simplest form of essay, description is not always a simple matter since the student will sometimes have to decide which of several contrasting accounts to accept as most valid.

In general, essays that ask for discussion require more thought than descriptive essays. Consider, for example, the essay topics outlined above. Whereas the descriptive essay about the causes of the Second World War asks simply for description, the discursive one on the same topic requires rather more thought. This may mean, for example, that a student feels compelled to give reasons for accepting or rejecting various possible descriptions of the causes of the war.

Finally, the evaluative essay requires definite commitment on the part of the student who may be required by such a question to decide whether, for example, a theory is valid or useful; most often he will also have to give reasons for his conclusions.

*Comparison*
To these three varieties of essay topic might be added a fourth style of task – the comparison. Sometimes essays ask that you compare (or 'compare and contrast') two or more viewpoints or pieces of work.

(i)   Compare Mead's account of the causes of the Second World War with that given by D. G. Jones.
(ii)  Compare Darwin's account of the origin of species with that given in the Old Testament story of creation.
(iii) Compare and contrast the behaviourist account of the development of morality with the psychodynamic account.

Comparison can take place at the level of description, discussion or evaluation, depending on what it is that you are being asked to compare. A comparison of two contrasting plays by the same writer, might simply involve describing the various elements of the plays, the ways in which their plots unfold, their relationship to each other and to the rest of the playwright's work and so on, in a way that does not necessarily involve expressing a preference for either. On the other hand, a comparison of two theories about the origin of the universe, for example, might require a detailed analysis and evaluation of evidence that might lead you to favour one over the other. Some essays which ask for comparison might legitimately be approached at more than one level. For example, the comparison between different accounts of the causes of the Second World War could be dealt with purely descriptively but might just as legitimately be dealt with in a more analytic and evaluative way. To some extent which of these a student chose would depend upon the way in which he had been taught and his knowledge of the expectations of his lecturers.

In a way this categorization of essay questions and topics in terms of description, discussion, evaluation and comparison is rather contrived. Though it does reflect the way in which essay-type tasks are very often formulated or worded, the expectations in each case are, in truth, less distinct than this categorization implies. So, for example, some cases of description will require the student to show that he is aware that alternative descriptions are possible and to give reasons for accepting one rather than another – in the same way that a discursive or an evaluative essay might. For example, given the nature of their subject matter, the essay titles 'Describe the origins of the universe' or 'Describe the way in which children develop language' clearly demand a discussion and evaluation of competing theories.

# 2.3 Approaching a piece of writing

Having said a little about some of the different sorts or writing that may be expected of students, we want now to turn to a consideration of some contrasting ways of approaching the task of writing as a student.

Some people find that for them the best approach to writing is to plan carefully and then write a draft at one sitting with all necessary references ready to hand. Others may find that the best way to begin is to write an immediate response to the question or topic without much initial planning. Then they may re-read it with the intention of striking out what is irrelevant and pinpointing what is important or interesting and should be extended. Either method is worth trying. What is important is that you get a first draft of your essay written as early as possible, even if this is little more than a full plan. Once you have a draft you can improve on it in successive revisions. It is no good reading enormous amounts of background material, making copious notes, and being so overwhelmed by what *might* be said that it becomes impossible to decide what *should* be said.

You may be advised to approach writing with the intention to 'Think, plan, write and revise'. This is sound advice. For many if not most writers, writing is a process in which they move between these various stages gradually developing a coherent way of presenting their views.

Some writers find that a rigid step-by-step approach suits them best and 'Think, plan, write and revise', in that order. They begin any piece of writing by thinking and planning; then they write a first draft which they revise as many times as necessary. However, others find that a more flexible approach suits them better.

Let us now have a look in a little more detail at what each of these two approaches might look like.

## A highly structured approach to writing

If you decide to use a structured approach to writing you may find it helpful to prepare a topic outline before writing a first draft. This can help you both to ensure that you have covered all relevant points and to avoid repetition. Preparing an outline can also be helpful in working out the best order in which to present ideas.

In preparing an outline consider carefully what you want to say about the topic. How should you best introduce what you want to say? How will you conclude? What are the central points of your argument? Each word should add something to the sense of the sentence and each sentence should add something to the thrust of the paragraph of which it is a part. Each paragraph should make a coherent contribution to what you write about your topic.

(i)   Begin by thinking about what it is you want to say including what conclusions you wish to reach. Write down a brief statement of the gist of what you intend to communicate, perhaps listing the main points to be made.

(ii)  Work out the best order for presenting your main points. Make a skeleton of your essay.

(iii) Check that the ideas you want to present follow on from one another. If they don't, add linking ideas.

(iv)  Check whether any examples you have listed are adequate to illustrate the main points you wish to make.

(v)   Decide on how you will introduce your essay. Write the draft introduction. Avoid longwindedness: introductions should do no more than engage the reader by giving some kind of 'trailer' for what is to come.

(vi)  Write a draft of the remainder of the essay.

(vii) Write the conclusion or concluding paragraphs. At this point you may wish to emphasize some points or recapitulate on the main threads in your argument; or you may wish to indicate areas into which you have not entered because to do so would have taken more space than you have had available. However, just as you should avoid longwindedness in the introduction, you should ensure that your concluding remarks do not waste your reader's time by simply repeating what is said elsewhere. Paradoxically, it will often be worth thinking about what you wish to conclude before even beginning to set pen to paper in preparing your initial plan, since this might influence what you decide to include and exclude from the main body of your essay.

You may find it easier to reverse (vi) and (v). Sometimes writing an introduction before the remainder of an essay leads one to give a summary of what is to come which will often be to waste valuable space.

## A less rigid approach

Someone who adopts a less rigid approach to writing might sit at a computer or with a piece of paper and pen and write freely for some time allowing ideas to pour out spontaneously. Often she will find that as she does this a plan of action begins to form in her mind and will jot this down as she goes along. Then she will re-read what she has written, tidy it up, and move ideas about into some kind of rough draft. Each time she returns to the work she will fill out sections as she is able, often as the result of reading or thinking done away from the piece in question.

In this less rigid approach it is still important to ensure that you have presented your ideas in a logical order, that your essay is coherent, that you have said all that is necessary to answer the question using adequate illustrations where necessary, and that your introduction and conclusion do their job well. As with a more highly structured approach you should make sure that each word, each sentence and each paragraph plays an important part in your essay.

## A spectrum of approaches

Between these two approaches there is a whole range of variations. You may write a few notes before attempting a relatively spontaneous first draft. You may begin by writing quite spontaneously the first thoughts that come to mind on a topic then use these in formulating a detailed plan. Or you may plan out some sections of your work quite carefully but work on the introduction and conclusion in a more spontaneous way.

One of us adopts a more methodical approach and the other a more spontaneous approach to writing. When we were working on this book the latter encountered a certain amount of difficulty in producing first drafts. It took him some time to realize that this was because of the rather rigorous planning that had gone into setting out the expected shape of the book with a list of main points to be made in each chapter, the order of chapters decided upon and so on. Rather than being helpful, he found that having an overall plan together with lists of ideas that should be incorporated into chapters actually constrained his ability to write. When eventually he just sat down and began to write about the ideas he had for the book in a more general way, he found that his ability to write came back fairly rapidly. He also discovered that his co-author was willing to look favourably on his efforts even to the extent of changing the overall structure of the book. If the approach you are using at any time does not seem to be helping you to write, try something else. If writing in a rigorously structured way doesn't work, try writing in a more free and spontaneous way. On the other hand if usually you write spontaneously but this is not working, if, say, you find that you are not writing anything that you find satisfactory, try writing some notes about what you want to say and organizing these into a possible plan for your essay.

We do not wish to advocate a more or less structured approach as being the best one. What is important for you, as it is for us, is that you find an approach that suits you. It is probably worth trying a variety of approaches and finding which works best. It may be that you will find more and less methodical approaches useful on different occasions. Remember, however, that thought, planning and revision are always important if you hope to write well whether you plan rigorously before you begin to write or rather lay your plans as you progress with your writing tasks.

Whatever approach you adopt it is as well to keep these questions in mind as you write:

What am I trying to communicate?

Where should I begin?

Where should I end?

Don't worry if you can't answer all of these questions when you begin writing your first draft. Keep them in mind as you write.

Whatever approach you adopt, in relation to each page and each paragraph it is worth asking yourself 'How does this help to answer the question I am addressing or to fulfil the task set?' If the section in question does not obviously add anything you should omit it. One of the worst pitfalls for any writer in attaining clarity and directness is the temptation to leave in material that is irrelevant or only marginally relevant to the topic. It is necessary to develop a ruthless streak in cutting out material that does not help to answer the question even when it is of great interest to you as a thinker or when you find that you have expressed yourself in a way that you find pleasing. One consolation to keep in mind as you press the delete key on your word processor, apply the liquid paper, or begin snipping with your scissors at some irrelevant but interesting section is that good ideas can often be used in other places.

Again, whatever approach you adopt, it is important to remember that the first paragraph of your essay introduces those who are reading it not only to your topic, but to you as a writer. You should aim in this first encounter with your reader to engage and interest (even excite) her and convince her that it will be worthwhile reading further. When she gets to the end of your concluding paragraph she should feel that the time she has devoted to your work was time well spent. If you achieve this you are likely to attain a good grade whether or not what you have written agrees with the reader's own views, whether you have included everything you could have done, whether you have made every learned reference you could have done. Your job as a writer is to interest your reader and convince her that you have thought deeply about the question. Some readers may be impressed if you show how much you remember of your lectures and how much you have read on the topic. All will be impressed if you show you have thought about it.

# 2.4 Sorting out what you have to say

When we are writing, just as when we are speaking, the very least we can hope to achieve is to make what we say or write coherent. This may sound obvious but it is not easy to achieve, particularly when we are not really clear about what it is that we are trying to say.

Labov (1969) reports a conversation in which a character known as Charles M. is asked 'Do you know of anything that someone can do, to have someone who has passed on visit him in a dream?' His reply may be thought of as a case where someone is not really clear about what he is trying to say:

> Well, I even heard my parents say that there is such a thing as something in dreams some things like that, and sometimes dreams do come true. I have personally never had a dream come true. I've never dreamt that somebody was dying and they actually died, or that I was going to have ten dollars the next day and somehow I got ten dollars in my pocket. I don't particularly believe in that, I don't think it's true. I do feel, though that there is such a thing as – ah – witchcraft, or some sort of *science* of witchcraft; I don't think that it's just a matter of believing hard enough that there is such a thing as witchcraft. I do believe that there is such a thing that a person can put himself in a state

of *mind*, or that – er – something could be given them to intoxicate them in a certain – to – to a certain – to a certain frame of mind – that – that could actually be considered witchcraft.

(Labov 1969, pp. 197–8)

At first glance it may look as if Charles M. doesn't know what he is trying to say. However, it is worth noting that Labov is reporting a contribution to a conversation rather than a piece of written prose. When this is taken into account it is easier to view Charles sympathetically. Like everyone who is involved in a conversation, especially one in which they are asked difficult questions about which they have not thought before, he is 'thinking on his feet' – trying to make sense in strange territory. We shall look at this example more fully in Section 3.3 where we will show how, by taking a sympathetic approach to trying to understand Charles, it can be seen that he may be saying something sensible, albeit in a rather muddled way.

In some instances the incoherent nature of what a person says or writes may suggest the possibility that not only have they not sorted out what they want to say but that they do not have very much to say. This possibility is well illustrated by the following extract from a speech made by a senior American politician:

I suppose three important things certainly come to mind that we want to say thank you. The first would be our family. Your family, my family – which is composed of an immediate family of a wife and three children, a larger family with grandparents and aunts and uncles. We all have our family whatever that may be . . . time and again I'm often reminded, especially in this presidential campaign, of the importance of a family, and what a family means to this country. And so when you pay thanks I suppose the first thing that would come to mind would be to thank the Lord for the family.
(Cited by Douglas Jehl in his article 'Family man Dan goes rambling for Thanksgiving', *Guardian*, 8 November 1988, p. 24, col. 7.)

Jehl further cites Quayle as wanting to 'thank you for the opportunities, and to thank you for the future, and to thank you for the past of what He has given us' (Jehl, op. cit.).

Jehl was drawing attention to the importance, for a high-level politician (the article was written during Senator Dan Quayle's campaign for Vice-President of the United States alongside George Bush), of being properly prepared before any speaking engagement, especially when his speech is part of an important campaign. As a student the demands upon you in terms of contribution to debate in, for example, a seminar or tutorial, are hardly likely to be as stringent as those that will be made upon a Presidential candidate. In your writing things are different. Since when you write you have more time to think, your lecturers will have higher expectations, especially when you have had some time in which to prepare an essay or seminar paper. You should therefore always think carefully about what you want to say before you try to say it, both when you speak and, more importantly, when you write.

As a general rule you are unlikely to write anything intelligible unless you have a clear idea of what you want to say. Even then it is not enough to know what you wish to say; what you wish to say needs to be reasonably consistent and put in such a way that the reader can understand what you are getting at.

Often writers can give the impression that they have something to say which is of profound importance; they do this, for example, by using important sounding words and phrases, making references to literature and the liberal use of metaphor. Consider, for example, the following passage cited by George Orwell:

> If a new spirit *is* to be infused into this old country, there is one thorny and contentious reform which must be tackled, and that is the humanization and galvanization of the BBC. Timidity here will bespeak canker and atrophy of the soul. The heart of Britain may be sound and of strong beat, for instance, but the British lion's roar at present is like that of Bottom in Shakespeare's *Midsummer Night's Dream* – as gentle as any sucking dove. A virile new Britain cannot continue indefinitely to be traduced in the eyes, or rather ears, of the world by the effete langours of Langham Place, brazenly masquerading as 'standard English'. When the Voice of Britain is heard at nine o'clock, better far and infinitely less ludicrous to hear aitches honestly dropped than the present priggish, inflated, inhibited, schoolma'amish arch braying of blameless, bashful, mewing maidens!
>
> (Letter in *Tribune* cited in Orwell 1968, Vol. 4, p. 158)

It seems to us that the author of this passage is ambiguous in what he says. The more natural interpretation is to think that he is arguing that the way in which the English language is spoken at the BBC is rather out of touch with the way in which it is spoken elsewhere. However, he could also be interpreted as arguing in favour of the use of non-standard English; in this case it seems particularly odd that in a passage arguing in favour of common language, he should use so many fanciful, even pompous, turns of phrase.

George Orwell is clearly less willing to forgive than we are. Discussing this passage, he writes: 'words and meaning have almost parted company. People who write in this manner usually have a general emotional meaning – they dislike one thing and want to express solidarity with another – but they are not interested in the detail of what they are saying' (op. cit. p. 164)

The following passage has the appearance of academic rigour and scholarly content and yet we can make very little of it. It has some similarity in emotion and level of commitment to the passage cited by Orwell.

Notice the use of words drawn from Latin and Greek and the somewhat abstruse scholarly references:

> Education is to do with educing, with releasing, with liberating. It would seem to do with the free and animated play of mind over experienced phenomena. Educating Rita is not training her; it is essentially releasing her into the life of thought and, therefore, existential possibility. It is no accident that the word 'school' derives from the Greek word 'schole' meaning both leisure (freedom from necessity) and discussion; freedom we might say, for discourse. It is pertinent that the word 'academy' derives from Akademus, the man who owned the garden/grove in which Plato and his students discussed philosophy. The metaphor of the garden – a protected place where utile pressure is off, where the mind can struggle to think its own thoughts – gives an essential resonance to this cluster of key words; education, school, academy. Certainly education bears within it the distinct resonance of transcendence.
>
> (Peter Abbs, 'Training Spells the Death of Education',
> *Guardian*, 5.1.87)

*Exercise*
Try to work out what Abbs is trying to say in this passage. It might be worthwhile trying to write the passage in your own words; in doing this try to capture the general flavour of what he is saying rather than trying to translate each word and phrase.

In Part 3 we argue in favour of adopting a generous approach when reading what others have written. This seems to us to be the best way of approaching written material and we have approached Abbs's passage with the intention of being as generous as possible. Even so, however, we can still make very little of it.

To be fair to Abbs the passage does convey meaning; it is just that the meaning is rather clouded by the language he uses. He seems to believe that schools and teaching should be about enabling students to think for themselves and that thus, in some sense, that it should be about giving them freedom to determine their lives. In our opinion he would have done well to have thought more clearly about what exactly he wanted to say before beginning to write. Having done that he could probably have said what he wanted to say more clearly by using simpler language, avoiding the use of unusual words such as 'utile' and vague phrases such as 'an essential resonance' and 'the distinct resonance of transcendence'.

Before you write anything as a student, you should take care to work out what it is that you want to say. Failing to do so may result in your writing something which says very little, takes too long to say what you want to say, or says it in a way that is unappealing and difficult to understand.

# 2.5  Drafting and revising

Writing is a difficult task. Very few people have the ability to write an essay at one sitting in a form that is adequate. If you want to write well you should be prepared to write several drafts and to revise each carefully. At each stage you should critically re-read what you have written, ensure that you have adequately addressed the topic, that your use of language is as good as you can make it and that you have not made any mistakes relating to spelling or grammar.

As you read ask yourself questions such as these:

Does my essay communicate what I intended to communicate?

Have I answered the question or carried out the task accurately?

Have I made all of the points that are necessary to support my views?

Is any of what I have written irrelevant?

Do I repeat myself unnecessarily?

Is my essay coherent? Are connections well made?

In reading and revising your work keep in mind questions such as these:

Who? What? Why? Where? When? How?

Robert Barrass (1982, p. 42) refers to these questions as 'mental tin openers'. By asking them you will locate areas of your work where more explanation or information is necessary.

As you work on writing each successive draft you may find that new ideas occur to you. Either write them down in a notebook or include them in the draft. Then in revising the draft locate the best place to include these ideas or decide that, however interesting they are, they are best left out. It is a good idea, if you can do it, to get someone else to type the final version of an essay because in trying to give birth to a piece of writing it is very tempting to make last-minute alterations to style and content; this can be disastrous.

If possible, as you complete each successive draft, get someone else to read it for you. Getting someone who is unfamiliar with your work to read it will give you an indication of whether you have been successful in communicating what you intended to communicate. This person should be someone who knows you well enough to be frank without giving offence. If such a person is not available, try entering dramatically into reading your own work as if you are someone else. This is difficult because familiarity with your work might mean that you are tempted to skip over some sections because you know them so well. You need, therefore, to learn to read your own work as if it belongs to someone else (as if you find it interesting, even when you are sick to death of its subject matter), and to be honest in appraising it. This is, incidentally, a good time to become aware of difficulties with style; being very closely involved with the writing yourself sometimes makes it difficult to see a stylistic infelicity or even a howler.

Ask your friend to point out places where your work is unclear, badly phrased, or repetitive. She can also point out obvious (or possible) errors in spelling and punctuation and check that you have fulfilled promises that you have made. For example, if you have written, 'I will argue that . . .', she should check that you have offered an argument; and if you have said that you will enter into more detail about a point later in your essay, she should check that you have done so. Your friend should also check that you have covered all points that you claim to have made and given all arguments that you claim to have given. For example, if in your conclusion you have written 'I have argued that . . .' she should ensure that you have indeed argued in favour of your position rather than simply *stating* it in the hope that your readers will go along with you. Your friend should also attend to places where you have employed phrases like: 'It follows from this that . . .' and 'This leads me into a discussion of . . .' and so on. Though such phrases can perform a useful function, they are often inserted in order to give the appearance of planning and structure, of cohesiveness and logicality where none of these exists. It is as well to take care to check that if you have used such phrases, you have actually done or are going to do what they claim you have done, or are going to do.

## Scissors, Sellotape and the word processor

In drafting and redrafting your work you should use the best technology available to you. Basically this means one of two things: a typewriter (with a decent ribbon), pen, scissors, Sellotape, correcting fluid and lots of energy for retyping, or a word processor.

Editing your work is essential to producing a good product. In editing you must avoid developing too much attachment to the words you have written. Just because they have come out of your head does not make them somehow sacred. They are there to be used if they do the job you intend them to; and they are there to be discarded if they do not. Whatever method of word processing you use it is essential to revise your work carefully if you want to produce a piece of work of which you will be proud.

In the 'scissors and Sellotape' method of word processing you should annotate the draft with which you are working with any changes you wish to make to the text including places where you want to rearrange it by moving sentences or even whole chunks about. You may want to write yourself notes about research that you now believe is necessary, for example, in pursuing references or facts that you want to have available before beginning on a new draft. Correcting fluid can come in handy for making minor changes to text, allowing you to remove text and write in changes more neatly. Do not be afraid to cut out words, phrases, even whole sections of text; even if they sound good or are interesting in themselves you should only leave them in if they help to answer the question. Write in any changed text above or, if necessary, on a fresh piece of paper which can then be Sellotaped over the old draft or, in the case of additional text, on a small flap of paper. When you have decided on a new form for your piece of writing and have done any necessary research, you should retype it before beginning the process again. If you have decided to move several chunks of text to different places you will probably find it useful to cut up the relevant pages and Sellotape them together in the new order before retyping.

Over the past few years it has become more and more common for people to have access to electronic word-processing facilities and it is very worthwhile trying to gain access to a word processor even if you can't afford to buy one. Word processing makes it easier to write well because it allows you to create and revise successive drafts without the tedious necessity of rewriting or retyping large chunks of text each time. A word processor allows you to move text about, delete and replace words, phrases, sentences and longer passages, in the same way as you would do in the scissors and Sellotape method. Its main advantages are that it permits you to edit your work faster and more easily and that you can keep a copy of the original text on disc in case you are unhappy with changes you make.

Don't let limited typing ability deter you from learning to use a word processor; the effort expended in learning to type adequately (this need not mean 'touch typing' – both of us type fairly quick;y and predomintly accruatelt usig lesd thsn a cmplete ste of figners) will be repaid many times over by the time you save in drafting and revising work and also by the ease with which it is possible to produce a piece of work that looks good. Nor should you allow computer phobia to deter you. Word processing is rather different from most uses of computers because it requires little if any technical knowledge in just the same way that driving a car does not require that one knows the first thing about the internal combustion engine. In some ways the word processor may be thought of as a glorified typewriter with a text storage facility and the ability to move, add and subtract text. However, to say this is perhaps to belittle the word processor.

A word processor allows you to create a piece of printed text using a standard keyboard rather like a typewriter. Rather than printing (or typing) characters directly onto a page, however, the word processor displays them on a screen (VDU or visual display unit) that looks like a television screen.

Having typed in a piece of text so that it is displayed on the screen a word processor allows you to do various things to it. For example, most word processors will allow you to delete words, phrases, sentences, paragraphs, or even larger sections, to move chunks of text around or copy them so that the same piece of text appears more than once. Some will allow you to check for spelling mistakes or at least to change particular spellings. Sometimes this can be a great boon. For example, one of us, who writes about medical and nursing ethics, frequently makes a typing error so that the word 'hospital' reads 'hostipal'. He can use his word processor to search within a section of text for all occurrences of 'hostipal' and replace them with 'hospital'; this saves a lot of time. However, a 'search-and-replace' facility can also have hilarious results if used carelessly. On one occasion the same author, writing something about special education, chose to refer to teachers as 'she' rather than 'he' – in order to avoid charges of sexism. Discovering several places where he had written 'he' rather than 'she' he used the search-and-replace facility in order to replace 'he' with 'she'. This resulted in some amusement when he discovered that a pair of co-authors named Cohen and Cohen turned out instead to be Coshen and Coshen while the words 'the' and 'there' turned into 'tshe' and 'tshere'.

A word processor is a relatively expensive item for a student to contemplate buying but it is an extremely worthwhile investment which will make writing a much less time-consuming activity. Because using a word processor will take much of the labour out of drafting and revising it will allow you to spend more time reading and thinking before you write each successive draft. Students who already use computers as part of their course, or who are learning about them for educational reasons as is the case with student teachers, would be foolish not to invest a little time in learning to use a word processor.

A word processor can help you to integrate all the stages of writing a piece of work. It will allow you to formulate a plan, fill in subheadings, complete first and subsequent drafts, and finally to print out a finished product with a minimum of fuss. The ease with which it is possible to delete and move text around using a word processor will allow you to be exploratory in your writing – trying a passage in several places before deciding where it should be placed, even if it should (at the flick of a key) be discarded. Before word processors were invented this was possible, of course, but as we have indicated above, it involved a great deal of paper, Sellotape, cutting, and making lines and annotations all over drafts. One of us remembers well sitting late into the night during the week prior to submitting a dissertation with several yards of typed script on odd pieces of paper Sellotaped together wondering how on earth he could decide whether it was finally ready to go to the typist. Many people, including those who are hesitant and lack confidence in writing, and also those who are meticulous and exacting and who spend the morning putting in a comma and the afternoon taking it out again, will benefit from the ease with which changes can be made to drafts using a word processor. A further advantage of a word processor is that it makes easier the business of changing successive drafts on the advice of friends or tutors who have read them for you.

Revising a piece of writing is partly about weeding out or amending ideas that are either marginal to the task in hand or mistaken. And it is partly about checking that the words used and the structure of the piece do the job of conveying meaning well. We want now to say something about structure and the crucial part it plays in communicating well in writing.

# 2.6 Attending to the needs of a readership

In Section 2.4 we discussed the importance of sorting out what you have to say before you speak, or more importantly before you write, as a student, by discussing some examples where it seems likely that the individuals in question had not done this. As well as becoming clear about what you want to say, it is necessary to think about your readers and about the best way of communicating with them.

As we pointed out in Section 1.1, most of the time when we write, we write for readers who will not be able to ask us questions about what we intended by what we have written. Important consequences follow from this, the most important of which is the need to attend to the clarity and coherence of what you write.

## The need for clarity

Since your reader cannot ask for clarification of your text, you need to ensure that what you write is clear. For example, you should make sure that there are no gaps in your text which prevent your reader from having a clear idea of what you are saying. You should avoid leaving out vital information, or referring back to something that you have omitted to mention in your text.

It is important to avoid ambiguity, that is, using expressions with more than one meaning. If, for example, someone writes 'Every boy loves some girl' it is left unclear as to whether she means that for every boy there is a girl that he loves, or that there is a particular girl who is loved by every boy. The expression 'All the nice girls love a sailor' leaves it unclear what is intended. One possible meaning is that all nice girls love all sailors though this seems somewhat strange since it is highly unlikely that all girls will know all sailors; less strange perhaps is the claim that all nice girls love sailors whoever they may be and that therefore every nice girl loves every sailor she sets eyes on. More plausibly it might mean that for every sailor there is a nice girl who loves him or that there is a particular sailor who is loved by all the nice girls.

Ambiguities of this kind should be avoided. In addition you must ensure that you are aware of the implications that follow from the assertions you wish to make. For example, the assertion 'All the nice girls love a sailor' carries with it the implication that any girl who doesn't love a sailor (or who doesn't love the sailor in question), can't be a nice girl.

Ambiguity often leads to amusement. Consider, for example, the story of the child who had lost a glove at school and who came home delighted a few days later and told her dad 'I found my glove walking up the corridor'; or the sign in a restaurant which proclaimed 'Patrons who think our waiters are rude should see the manager.'

Newspapers are a good source of amusing ambiguity. Consider, for example, the article in a local newspaper which began 'Brian kept his pigeons down the garden with his brother Sid'; or the advertisement offering a dog for sale which read 'Dog for sale. Will eat anything. Loves children.' Where, as in these examples, ambiguities are amusing, they are easy to spot. Unfortunately ambiguity is not always easy to detect and you should not assume that just because you know what you mean your audience will also know what you mean. Re-reading what you have written, or getting another person to read what you have written, will often be useful in detecting ambiguity. For example, an early draft of this book contained the sentence: 'Even when you are required to demon- strate certain knowledge, you should beware of simply regurgitating notes you have taken in lectures'. Because we knew what we intended this sentence to communicate we failed to notice the ambiguity in the word 'certain'. Whereas we had intended to say something about particular aspects of knowledge that students might be expected to demonstrate that they have, someone pointed out that it could be taken as referring to occasions when students have to demonstrate that the knowledge they have is certain in the sense that there can be no doubt about it. Be alert to the possibility that what you have written is capable of different interpre- tations.

Avoid writing in a particular regional dialect and stick to standard English wherever possible. In recent years it has become quite fashionable to recommend that children should be encouraged to write in the dialect with which they are most familiar. The reason advanced is that if it is not done children will think that their own way of speaking is being looked down upon and that they will, therefore, become alienated from school and its values.

There is no real evidence in favour of this view. What *would* be demeaning to a person's way of speaking would be to discourage or prevent her from speaking in her native dialect or language, as happened in relation to the speaking of Welsh in Wales in the nineteenth century. Provided that children are encouraged to use the form of speech or writing that is most appropriate to their needs at a particular time, there is no reason to suppose that the use of their own dialect, when appropriate, should not be encouraged; but this is not yet to say that children should be encouraged to use _____ language to the exclusion of a standard form.

There are so _____ a standard form when writing. Both _____ kers can read standard English. On _____ ect will be at ease reading it. This m _____ wider audience by writing in standard _____ dialect.

The use of a n _____ ambiguity. For example, in Yorkshire, it is qu _____ he way that 'until' would be used in standard _____ ay 'I'm waiting while school finishes' meaning _____ es'. In certain contexts, this use of 'while' could _____ es. For example, if a sign on a level crossing re _____ s are passing', a (foolish) Yorkshireman, una _____ glish, might interpret this as meaning that he sho _____ until the train arrives before attempting to cross.

In some parts of the country, the expression 'Everybody can't drive' means what is meant in standard English by 'Not everybody can drive'. However, it could plausibly mean a number of other things. For example, it could mean what 'Nobody can drive' means in standard English. Since everyone can understand 'Not everybody can drive' and since quite a few people will either regard 'Everybody can't drive' as ungrammatical or as meaning the equivalent of 'Nobody can drive', it would be better to use the expression 'Not everybody can drive' if we want to communicate the idea that driving is not a universal skill.

## The need for coherence

Not only should what you write be clear in its meaning, it should also make sense beyond the level of the statement; it should make sense as a text. This requirement is easier to state than it is to describe briefly. At the core of the idea of coherence is the need for the overall message or argument that you are conveying to hang together and be consistent. You should not contradict yourself either explicitly or implicitly.

To make the idea of coherence clearer, it may be helpful to consider an example. Suppose that a historian is writing an article, the central claim of which is that the Soviet Union was responsible for the outbreak of the Second World War; in other words that in some sense the Soviet Union caused the war. Her argument for this contention might involve the claim that divisions on the German Left allowed Hitler to come to power. In the course of this article she may assert, additionally, that Germany caused the outbreak of hostilities with the Soviet Union by invading Soviet territory in 1941. So she seems to be claiming both that the Soviet Union was responsible for the war and that Germany was responsible for it. Because of these apparently contradictory claims a critic may charge our historian with inconsistency. However, our historian may have anticipated such difficulties and taken account of them in developing her argument. One way in which she might have done this is by imagining what a critical readership, one which is only too ready to pick holes in what she has written, might have to say about her article. This is a very valuable exercise. Even if the target readership is not very critical, taking account of an imaginary critical readership is a very good discipline for an author who can then go some way towards anticipating what may be said in objection to her arguments.

Having taken account of what an imagined critical reader might have to say about her work our historian may avoid the accusation of inconsistency by distinguishing between various senses of 'cause'; in other words she may draw attention to the ambiguity of this word. She might point out, for example, that whereas the Soviet Union caused the war in the sense that its actions in interfering in German politics in the 1920s and 1930s were decisive in enabling Hitler's rise to power in Germany to take place, this is not inconsistent with the further claim that Germany's invasion of the Soviet Union caused the outbreak of hostilities between these two countries. However, the question of whether or not her argument is convincing, or even plausible, is not the point at issue here. What is important is that she has at least attempted to achieve clarity and maintain consistency in what she has written.

As we have already said, when you are reading you rely on the author to supply all the relevant information that you need to understand the text. This means that when you are writing, you need to be comprehensive in providing all that is needed for the reader to understand what you have written. As a writer you have a variety of sources of information available to you: your memory, files, notes, reference books and so on. One danger faced by an inexperienced writer is that of mistakenly assuming that since she has access to multiple sources of information, her readers also have them available. As a writer you can only assume that your readers have one source of information, namely what you have written. You therefore need to ensure that you include all important information in your text, even much that you think that a reasonably well-informed reader might well know. It is a useful exercise to read what you have written as if you were a novice in relation to the subject matter, to identify where a reader might fail to understand because vital information is not presented.

There is an important difference between providing adequate background to enable your readers to follow your line of thought or argument and insulting or patronizing them. You will not insult their intelligence by ensuring that they have access to important items of information. You may well do so by employing careless or facile arguments or by withholding vital information or references from them. To continue with our example of the Second World War, our historian may well wish to refer to the Comintern (the Third Communist International, the organization that effectively controlled the Communist parties of the inter-war period and was itself effectively controlled by the Soviet Union) and the political parties of the

Weimar Republic (the name given to the German State of the pre-Hitler period). If she does so, then she needs to ensure that her readers have all the necessary information about these organizations before she starts referring to them in developing her argument. Even is she is fairly sure that her readership is a knowledgeable and scholarly one, she should do this, for several reasons.

(i)     Although knowledgeable, they may not have the necessary detailed information at their fingertips.

(ii)    In setting out the information and the references, she is demonstrating to the reader that she knows what she is writing about. This is particularly important if her reader is a tutor who is, to a large extent, interested in her own grasp of the subject matter.

(iii)   Her readers may have differing levels of knowledge about her subject matter. Our historian needs to be able to reach the least knowledgeable of her target audience as well as the most knowledgeable.

Writing involves mental and physical effort; more so than does speaking. This means that one is very often reluctant to rewrite what one has already written. The skill of writing and rewriting is, however, one of the most important skills that the successful author can acquire. Its importance is such that many educationists now recommend that the arts of drafting and redrafting be practised by children in the primary school, let alone at the secondary and higher education levels. Indeed the art of drafting and revising is now part of the National Curriculum in our primary schools (DES and Welsh Office 1990). If you are producing a serious piece of writing that is intended to represent your best efforts, then you need to see the writing process as one that consists of several stages. These are likely to proceed from notes to drafts, that is, from concentrated and fragmentary sketches of what you wish to say, to passages of continuous and grammatical prose which are serious attempts to write what you want to write.

Satisfying the demands of consistency, coherence and comprehensiveness is not an easy task, particularly for the inexperienced writer. Drafting and redrafting is one way of attempting to satisfy these demands. You need to be prepared to read and re-read what you have written with the demands of your readers in mind and you need to have the patience to rewrite what you have written if those demands are not fully satisfied.

# 2.7 Structure and clarity

The way in which a piece of writing is structured is important in determining the extent to which it is successful in communicating. The order in which material is presented, the use of 'signposts' such as subheadings to help indicate the way in which ideas relate to one another, and the way in which it is set out, including the use of punctuation, can all make a difference to its success or failure. Lack of attention to structure can lead to a reader becoming hopelessly lost even in a relatively short essay.

## Arranging and organizing

Like elephants, meals and human lives, essays should have a beginning, a middle and an end. Some of the worst faults we have found in student essays occur when it is impossible to tell where they are leading or what their main points are. Your job as a writer is at least partly to help your reader to find her way round what you have written. Taking care over the way in which you arrange or organize the ideas, arguments and examples in your essay is one way in which you can do this.

In structuring your work you should try as far as possible to ensure that as she reads, your reader has the feeling that she knows where she is going, can remember where she has been, and can see how the section that she is currently reading relates to both. Unless you do this your reader can easily lose sight of even the most central ideas you are trying to present.

## Signposting

Offering signposts helps to make clear to your reader what you will be focusing on in major sections of your work. By 'signposts' we mean verbal or structural indications about the direction your argument or discussion is taking, analogous to the signposts one follows on the road.

Subheadings are one device you can use to tell your reader where you are going; they serve as a kind of signpost indicating the next point on her journey through your thoughts. So, for example, in discussing a play and its relationship to a playwright's other work, you might have subheadings such as these: 'The plot', 'The main characters', 'The relationship of the play to X's other work'. Or, writing an account of an experiment in science, you might employ subheadings such as: 'Hypotheses', 'Method', 'Results' and 'Conclusions'.

Though they are a useful tool in signposting, subheadings are not the only means available for guiding a reader through your work. At times it may be helpful to indicate where you are going by giving 'trailers' for what is to come and sometimes it may be useful to remind your readers where they have been, particularly when your argument is complex. For example, you may write 'I will argue that . . .' or 'I have suggested that . . .'. Both trailers and reminders, however, should be short and serve a useful purpose; they should not be simple repetitions of what is said elsewhere. Attending to signposts can help you to identify major sections for your essay, thus ensuring, for example, that you cover all parts of a question. They can also help in guarding against the possibility of including material that is irrelevant to the main thrust of the essay.

## Paragraphing

Arranging your writing in paragraphs breaks it up into manageable chunks. A new paragraph offers a chance for your reader to pause at an appropriate point in your writing and will usually signal a change in direction such as the entry of an important new idea or argument. Each paragraph can be thought of as a container for a separate point in a topic or argument and you should avoid beginning new paragraphs in the middle of closely connected streams of ideas.

Often students are uncertain about how long the paragraphs they write should be. To some extent the length of paragraphs is a matter of personal choice provided that the way in which your paragraph helps to communicate your meaning. Short paragraphs are likely to be easier to read than long ones and you should try to avoid very long paragraphs, particularly when you are writing something quite short like an essay. If in writing essays you find it difficult to cut paragraphs down to size, you may be writing at too great a level of detail for an essay. It might, in this case, be worth considering whether, for the purpose of the current task, you are including material that could be left out.

Another important aspect of structure is the way in which you use punctuation. This is dealt with in the next section.

# 2.8 Punctuation

Punctuation should help readers to understand what you intend to communicate. We punctuate in order to help the reader to understand our meaning. In speaking one pauses to show breaks in one's train of thought; in writing, the use of punctuation allows such natural breaks to be apparent to the reader. The use of punctuation can also help to indicate meanings that in speech would be conveyed by tone of voice, gesture, stress on particular words or syllables, pauses and so on. However, it can also cloud meaning especially where it is overused. We agree with Shoosmith (1928) who, in a book intended for pupils between the ages of 11 and 15, wrote, 'stops being of the nature of a disagreeable necessity, should be used as little as possible . . . and . . . only in so far as they are of assistance to the reader'. Would that our students had learned that punctuation is intended to serve a useful function; too many seem to use it rather like a kind of decorative embellishment.

In a book of this size we cannot begin to do justice to the issues raised by punctuation; for that you should consult a reliable text (see, for example, *Fowler's Modern English Usage*). What we can do, however, is to indicate the main punctuation devices that you should be able to employ and some of their more common uses. If you find punctuation difficult you will find it easiest to write short sentences if possible.

> Short sentences can lead to a boring style. However, this is no worse than being wrong. Perhaps it is better. It is for you to decide. In any event practice makes perfect. Start with short sentences. Then gradually as you become more confident, you can begin to use a more flowing style utilizing all the various punctuation marks; doing so will no doubt enhance the character of your written work, making it easier as well as less boring to read.

You should ensure that you are able to make correct use of the following: full stop, capital letters, comma, semi-colon, colon, question mark, exclamation mark, apostrophe, brackets, inverted commas and hyphen. You should also learn to paragraph appropriately and to use indentation to make certain sections of your work stand out. The use of the dash – for example, in making an aside – is also worth learning.


## The full stop

The full stop (.) marks the longest pause and is used to mark the end of a sentence, unless the sentence is a question or an exclamation. It is also used with shortened forms of words and abbreviations.

Shortened forms of words that end in the same letter as the full word do not usually require a full stop, for example, Mr (Mister) and Dr (Doctor). However, shortened forms of words that do not end in the same letter as the full word do require a full stop, for example, Rev. (Reverend) and Oct. (October). Strictly speaking, whereas Rev. and Oct. are abbreviations, Mr and Dr are contractions because they result from leaving out the middle of the word.

Full stops are sometimes used to indicate abbreviation of groups of words as, for example, in G.C.S.E for 'General Certificate of Secondary Education', M.P. for 'Member of Parliament' and N.E.W.I. for 'North East Wales Institute'. Nowadays, however, it is most common to write abbreviations consisting of capital letters without full stops. Thus we would write GCSE, MP and NEWI, and also BBC (British Broadcasting Corporation), EC (European Community) and BA (Bachelor of Arts). However, full stops are usually retained in abbreviations that include lower-case letters, such as M.Ed. (Master of Education) and Ph.D. (Doctor of Philosophy).

Full stops are omitted in the case of acronyms (names formed from the initial letters of the separate words making up the name), for example, NATO for North Atlantic Treaty Organization and CCEDAR for the Clwyd Centre for Educational Development and Research. At times what might be called semi-acronyms are formed to give memorable labels for things of public concern. A recent example of this is the GERBILL ('great' Education Reform Bill) which introduced a new ERA (Education Reform Act) in English and Welsh Education in 1988.

It is best to avoid the use of abbreviations. However, if the use of an abbreviation is essential because, for example, what it stands for is more commonly known by an abbreviation or acronym than by its full name, or its name is cumbersome, then it is best to introduce the full name first of all, followed by the abbreviation or acronym in brackets. For example, organizations such as the United Nations International Children's Emergency Fund and the Society for the Protection of Unborn Children are more commonly known as UNICEF and SPUC. And the AA and the RAC are more commonly known by the words sounded by spelling their abbreviations aloud than as the Automobile Association and the Royal Automobile Club respectively. In such cases on the first occasion you refer to the organization in question you should again use its full name followed by the abbreviation in brackets; after that you can use the abbreviation. You should not assume that your readers will understand every abbreviation you use.

## *The question mark*

The question mark (?) is equivalent to the full stop in terms of the length of pause intended. It is used at the end of every sentence in which a question is asked in direct speech. For example,

'What time is it?' he asked.

Question marks should not be used in indirect speech, for example, in writing the sentence:

He asked what time it was.

## *The exclamation mark*

The exclamation mark (!) is also equivalent to the full stop in terms of the length of pause intended. It is used as a mark of emphasis. For example, we might write 'You should not use an exclamation mark except when you wish to emphasize a point!' In general it is probably a good idea to avoid the use of exclamation marks in writing essays. It is better to emphasize points by the use of emphatic language.

## *The comma*

The comma (,) is used to separate the elements of a list as in 'The main devices for indicating pauses in writing are the full stop, comma, semi-colon, colon, question mark and exclamation mark'. Notice, however, that the last two members of a list are usually separated by the conjunction 'and' rather than by a comma. Occasionally a comma as well as the conjunction will be necessary for the sake of clarity, for example, where the list contains elements that in themselves employ 'and':

> The menu, which consisted of rather greasy foods, included fish and chips, chicken and chips, sausage and chips, and bacon and chips.

The comma has many other uses which are too numerous to be treated exhaustively here. However, a case which frequently gives rise to confusion is their use in relation to *non-defining* as distinct from *defining* adjectival clauses. Consider the following two sentences which use the same words, punctuated differently, to make two different points:

(i)   The ambulance drivers in London, who were the first to strike, are the most anxious to begin work again.
(ii)  The ambulance drivers in London who were the first to strike are the most anxious to begin work again.

These two sentences use the same words and yet suggest different meanings.

The first of these sentences, (i), suggests both that the ambulance drivers in London began striking first, and that they were the most anxious of all ambulance drivers to begin working again. The adjectival clause 'who were the first to strike' is marked off from the main clause by commas and is said to be *non-defining*; it merely gives more information about the ambulance drivers. This sentence could be recast thus without changing its meaning:

> The ambulance drivers in London were the first to strike and they are the most anxious to begin work again.

The second sentence, (ii), implies that those drivers in London who came out on strike first were the first, within London, to want to return to work; the absence of commas shows that the adjectival clause 'who were the first to strike' is more indissolubly connected to the noun it qualifies. It specifies or *defines* which ambulance drivers in London we are talking about. Consequently it cannot be omitted without significantly altering the meaning of the sentence.

Nowadays the comma is frequently used informally (and often rather too frequently) to indicate natural pauses and to separate distinct parts of a sentence. It is rather difficult to give advice on the use of commas to indicate pauses since to some extent how they are used depends upon the way in which a writer would read a sentence were she to read it out loud. However, you should take note of the danger inherent in this informal use of commas which is that it can lead to overuse and consequently a lack of clarity. In general commas should be used to indicate a pause only where this is not obvious from the sense of the words or where its use actually changes the sense of the words.

## The semi-colon

The semi-colon (;) indicates a pause which, while considerably longer than that indicated by a comma, is less than that indicated by a full stop. It may be used to divide the components of compound sentences; these usually have a strong connection with one another. In this context it often takes the place of 'and' or 'but'; its use can give a smoother effect than a series of full stops. For example:

> Both trailers and reminders, however, should be short and serve a useful purpose; they should not be simple repetitions of what is said elsewhere.

> In a book of this size we cannot begin to do justice to the issues raised by punctuation; for that you should consult a reliable text.

Sometimes semi-colons are used to separate long, self-contained sections of a sentence. For example:

> I am not suggesting that whenever a patient thinks that her life isn't worth living any longer and asks to be killed, that her doctor should kill her; to say this would be to suggest that anyone who is depressed with life has the right to be killed and I certainly don't believe that.

The semi-colon is also used to separate the elements of a list where the elements themselves contain commas and to use commas would thus cause confusion. For example:

> The modern symphony orchestra consists of several groups of related instruments including violins, violas, cellos and basses in the strings; flutes, clarinets, oboes and bassoons in the woodwind; trumpets, horns, trombones and tuba in the brass, as well as the wide range of instruments in the percussion section.

## The colon

The colon (:) indicates a change in meaning that is more abrupt than that indicated by a semi-colon. It has several uses.

(i)    It may be used to introduce examples. (We have been using it in this way throughout this section of the book). For example:

Lots of flowers appear in spring. For example: snowdrops, crocuses, daffodils and primroses.

(ii)   It may be used where you want to introduce a clause which amplifies or explains a previous sentence. For example:

There were two reasons for his success as a novelist: the first was his innate talent as a storyteller, the second was the high level of commitment he put into researching the material for his books.

(iii)  The colon may be used to introduce lists. For example:

The ingredients for pineapple surprise pudding are: one medium pineapple, three tablespoons of Greek yoghurt, one fresh egg, one tablespoon of honey, freshly ground roasted almonds . . .

(iv)   Finally the colon may be used to introduce a quotation which does not follow naturally on from a word such as 'said' or 'wrote'. For example:

The idea that we should do unto others as we would like them to do unto us, finds expression in many places including, for example, the sayings of Confucius: 'What you do not like when done to yourself, do not do to others.'

## Brackets

Brackets ( ) are used to indicate an aside from the main train of thought, most often within a sentence. Sometimes brackets are known as 'parentheses' although strictly speaking a parenthesis is an aside which may be indicated using brackets, dashes or commas. For example:

This alternative would have the benefit over the last, that doctors would not put (and could not be accused of putting) ideas into the heads of those who were satisfied with their lives.

In this case the brackets serve to interject something that might otherwise have formed the basis of another sentence. Sometimes brackets are used to enclose a whole sentence to show that it is an aside from the main train of thought. For example, on page 59 we write:

Sometimes students develop the habit of putting inverted commas round a word with which they feel uncomfortable, or when they are unsure that it is the correct word to use. (In this context inverted commas are often known as 'scare quotes'.) For example one of our students . . .

Sometimes brackets are used to inject a humorous remark into a sentence though we would advise that you avoid this unless it serves to make a point that reinforces the position you are putting forward.

## The dash

The dash (–) is a useful punctuation mark though many people disapprove of its use. It is useful in performing a function similar to, but different from, that performed by brackets in indicating an aside and sometimes people simply use dashes in place of brackets. However, they are more often used to emphasize a point or to make it stand out than to interject a separate idea. The use of dashes serves to isolate a point from the main thrust of a sentence rather less than the use of brackets. For example:

> The microwave – whether you like it or not – is now so well accepted that it is considered almost indispensable by many cooks.

The dash can also be used in place of a semi-colon as in the sentence 'When he finally stood up from the dinner table he felt distinctly woozy – the world was going round and round'. There is an immediacy about this sentence – a sense of connection between the two clauses – that would be missing if a semi-colon had been used.


## *The apostrophe*

The apostrophe (') has two uses. First, it is used to indicate possession. There are several conventions. In the case of singular nouns, and plural nouns not ending in s, it is customary to add 's. Thus, for example, we would write Tom's or Dick's car and women's or children's rights. On the other hand, in the case of plurals that end in s, it is conventional to add only the apostrophe, hence we would write: girls' toys and boys' bags. The apostrophe could also be used by itself in the case of words such as 'Moses' or 'thesis' where it would sound inelegant to indicate a possession by adding 's. Thus, for example, we might refer to Moses' wife and to a thesis' contents rather than to Moses's wife and the thesis's contents. Better still, in the latter case, would be to use a different form of words and refer to 'the contents of the thesis'.

In the case of multiple-noun possessives you should add the apostrophe to the last noun only: Fortnum and Mason's delicatessen counter. In the case of compound nouns the possessive is formed by adding the apostrophe to the last word: brother-in-law's.

The other common use of the apostrophe is to denote contractions. This is most common in colloquial English, for example, in the words *don't, can't* and *couldn't* where the apostrophe stands for the missing letter 'o'. In some other uses the apostrophe indicates the absence of more than one letter. This is the case, for example, in we'd, we'll and shan't (which if written accurately according to the conventions would read sha'n't), the full forms of which would be respectively, *we would, we will* and *shall not*. Without the use of the apostrophe 'two o'clock' would read 'two of the clock'. Finally the apostrophe may be used in referring to dates, for example, to the summer of '76.

Take special note that the apostrophe is only very rarely used in forming plurals. For example, the plural of 'cat' is 'cats' not 'cat's'; and the plural of 'computer' is 'computers' and not 'computer's'. Notice, however, the use of the apostrophe in forming plurals in the phrase 'mind your p's and q's'.


## Inverted commas

Inverted commas (" or "") are used to indicate direct speech and to indicate quotation. For example:

(i)   The witness said, 'I saw the thief running into the pub, your honour'.
(ii)  'What time is it?' he asked.
(iii) 'This', said the teacher, writing furiously on the blackboard, 'is the correct way to use inverted commas'.
(iv)  Fairbairn and Winch (1991) write: 'Like elephants, meals and human lives, essays should have a beginning, a middle and an end'.

Often when longer passages are quoted directly quotation marks are omitted and the passage is indented on the next line; in such circumstances the quoted words are often introduced by a colon. See, for example, the way in which we introduce the quotation from Dan Quayle on page 38 or the way in which we introduce a quotation from a student essay in which the student is referring to the work of Wittgenstein, below. There is no rule about how long a passage has to be to be dealt with in this way, though we would suggest that if you are quoting more than about two lines you should consider indentation.

Where direct speech or a quotation is introduced by a saying verb such as 'said', 'asserted' or 'wrote', you should use a comma or colon after the saying verb; see, for example, examples (i) and (iv) above. You should also use a comma before the direct speech if it continues after a subordinate clause, as in (iii) above.

The question of whether to use single or double inverted commas is to some extent a matter of taste. Even publishers adopt different conventions. For example, whereas some publishers, including the Open University Press who published this book, use single quotation marks (') except for quotes within quotes, other publishers use double quotation marks ("") except for quotes within quotes. What is important is that you take account of the possibility that you might wish to quote material that has direct speech within it, or (which is less likely), to use direct speech in which someone quotes from some other source.

For example, a philosophy student writing an essay about language, referred to some of Wittgenstein's remarks in the Blue and Brown Books:

Wittgenstein raised the problem of ostensive definition in a memorable way in the Blue and Brown Books: 'The questions "What is length?", "What is meaning?", "What is the number one?" etc., produce in us a mental cramp. We feel that we can't do anything in reply to them and yet ought to point to something.'

(Wittgenstein 1958)

As an example of the use of direct speech in which someone quotes from another source we might mention the schoolteacher, taking a class in personal, social and moral education who asked 'What do you think that St Augustine meant when he wrote "Lord make me chaste – but not now"?'

Sometimes inverted commas are used to indicate that one is referring to a term rather than using it. For example:

> The term 'abortion' has two distinct uses. On the one hand it is used to refer to the natural miscarriage of a baby before twenty-eight weeks gestation. On the other it is used to refer to the premature ending of a pregnancy by deliberate intervention.

Sometimes students develop the habit of putting inverted commas round a word with which they feel uncomfortable, or when they are unsure that it is the correct word to use. (In this context inverted commas are often known as 'scare quotes'.) For example, one of our students recently wrote:

> . . . the theory is structured on a 'model', as with many theories of economics, and within the 'model' assumptions are established.

This student is using inverted commas round the word 'model' to indicate, not that he is referring to the word rather than using it but to indicate his uncertainty or nervousness about whether it is the appropriate word.

Another student used scare quotes in discussing an individual, said to have been indoctrinated, who had shaken off the beliefs in which she was supposed to have been indoctrinated: '. . . she has effectively "shook off" her unshakeable beliefs . . .'. The use of scare quotes here suggests that the student was unsure whether he should have been writing 'shook off' or rather 'shaken off'; not to have checked gave a bad impression to the examiner.

Using scare quotes like this is a habit which you should avoid forming; it is far better to search carefully for words about which you do feel confident and which express your meaning as precisely as possible. There are, however, occasions when it might be acceptable to place a word within inverted commas to indicate some unease one has about using it. For example, someone who does not subscribe to the view that madness is the result of illness, may reinforce her opinion that there is no such thing as mental illness by putting inverted commas round the term 'mental illness' whenever she uses it.

The use of scare quotes is related to the use of what Anthony Flew (1976) refers to as 'sneer quotes' when one is using a word sardonically, when one wishes to indicate that one thinks that another's use of a term is unjustified or to sneer at or ridicule its use.

## Capital letters

Capital letters (A, B, C, D . . .) are the first punctuation devices that children meet in school. Capital letters are used at the beginning of sentences. Capitals are also used for the names of people, places, organizations, the days of the week, months of the year and for titles (for example, the Prime Minister, the Queen, the Archbishop of York). Capitals are used for the adjectives which derive from the names of countries, such as French, German and Dutch. They are used in many, but not all, abbreviations. If the words for which the abbreviation stands would have been given capitals then the abbreviation is written using capitals. Thus, for example, we write UNICEF and MP. If the words would not have been written using capitals we do not use them in the abbreviated form. Thus, p.m. and e.g. are written in lower-case letters. You should avoid using capitals unnecessarily. For example, queen and bishop are usually only written using capital letters when they are part of a person's title, otherwise they are common nouns; and God is usually only given a capital when we are referring to the one God not to a collection of gods.

## The hyphen

The hyphen (-) is used in several different ways though its use is becoming less common and you should consult a reliable and up-to-date dictionary if you are unsure whether one is necessary. (See, for example, The Shorter Oxford English Dictionary.) For example, it is used to link together the elements of compound words such as son-in-law and to link together words which, when joined, have a special meaning, for example, best-seller and dry-clean. Another use is in words such as re-cover and re-sign where without the hyphen an entirely different meaning would be conveyed. A footballer who re-signs has not resigned and a person who recovers his Victorian chaise longue after it was stolen may or may not, have it re-covered.

## Punctuation can change meaning

Punctuation can help you to communicate both accurately and elegantly. We have discussed the most common punctuation devices that are in use. It is important that you learn to use them appropriately if you want to develop as a writer.

Let us end with a warning: the way in which we punctuate can entirely change the meanings we convey. This means that it is important to exercise great care in punctuating your work. For example, consider the following string of words:

> The teacher said the girl is very silly'

The meaning of this group of words is entirely different depending on the punctuation used:

> 'The teacher', said the girl, 'is very silly'.

> The teacher said, 'The girl is very silly'.

Or consider the following:

> 'When we arrived at the restaurant we met Alex and his brother Sam joined us later.'

This sentence implies that the speaker and his companions met Alex at the restaurant and that they were joined later by Alex's brother who is called Sam. It could be made more clear by substituting a semi-colon for the conjunction 'and'.

> 'When we arrived at the restaurant we met Alex; his brother Sam joined us later.'

By changing the punctuation slightly we can completely change the sense of the sentence:

> 'When we arrived at the restaurant we met Alex and his brother; Sam joined us later.'

Here we learn that when they arrived at the restaurant the speaker and his companions met Alex and his brother and that Sam joined them later.

These examples are rather amusing and unusual ones. However, it is easy to find examples from the work of students where lack of attention to punctuation has caused problems in meaning, even rendering groups of words meaningless. We suggest that you look for such examples in your own work and remove them.

# 2.9 Word limits and the responsibilities of the author

When you have a limited number of words available it is likely that you will find it necessary to omit much that is relevant. Part of the skill in writing essays is in deciding what is essential and what inessential to the answer you wish to give from the relevant material you have at hand. In order to stay within word limits you will often have to assume that certain ideas and arguments are familiar to your readers. However, you must remember that part of your task will often be to show that you understand ideas and arguments to which you have been introduced in classes. In order to decide which ideas you can use without explanation and which you must explain, you will have to think carefully about the main thrust or point of the question. Some questions more than others will be a test of what you know. Some will be more of a test of your ability to think through a problem for yourself. All will be a test of your ability to select appropriate material and to make decisions about what is centrally important in presenting a case.

Often students worry that within the word limits that are put upon essays they cannot say everything that they think is important. This is understandable; most people who write professionally have the same difficulty. But it is part of growing up as a writer that you have to learn to take responsibility for what you leave in and what you leave out of your written work. Of course in marking work at both undergraduate and postgraduate level lecturers may write things of this kind in the margin: 'This is good as far as it goes, but I should like to have seen a discussion of . . .' or 'Really you should have pursued this point in more depth'. This is infuriating but inevitable; and unfortunately you can't really do much to change lecturers. However, the way you write can convince your readers that you have missed points out because you believe others to be more important rather than through ignorance or lack of thought. By writing concisely and making sure that everything you include in your essay is to the point, you can make all the difference to whether your reader believes that you have missed things out in order to stay within a certain word limit or rather because you don't know enough about your subject matter.

You must learn to cut out irrelevancies – odd phrases that add nothing to your essay; we could call such phrases 'essay fillers' in much the same way as retailers of children's toys talk about 'stocking fillers' at Christmas. We're referring here to phrases such as 'At this moment in time . . .' and 'This is precisely the point at issue'.

Avoid anything that is not essential to your answer. To do otherwise is to squander words that could be put to use in communicating what you wish to communicate. Phrases at the beginning of sentences can often by omitted without changing the point which is being made. Here we are thinking, for example, of phrases of this kind: 'It should of course, be noted that . . .' and 'With reference to . . . I should make the point that . . .'. Avoid statements such as 'This leads us on to a point which is essential to any adequate discussion of this topic'. This indicates little other than your belief that the point you are about to make is important. Including the point within the word limits you have been set would indicate just as clearly that you consider it important, without such a preamble. Phrases of this kind are often heard in discussion. For example, a television interviewer might ask an MP what the government intends to do about a financial problem. In answering she might begin: 'Well, at this moment in time, given the constraints under which we are operating and the very difficult situation in which we find ourselves, there seems to be no other way out of this very difficult situation than to increase the level of taxation'. Everything up until the point at which she said 'increase the level of taxation' is really a time filler. In a way this is excusable in a situation where a person is having to respond to a directly asked question. What's going on is that she is buying time to think. But it's inexcusable in writing because when we write we should think ahead and only write what actually communicates. It seems to us to be disrespectful of a reader to expect her to wade through a lot of verbiage before she gets to the point you're trying to make; in addition it's possible to miss the point totally if there's too much verbal junk around.

If you have to say what you're going to do, do it clearly and simply; don't make a meal of it. Saying what you're going to do can lead to repetition and is often a way of filling in space rather than performing a useful function.

# 2.10  Supporting your claims

In writing as a student you will be expected to demonstrate knowledge and thought; in doing so you will be expected also to offer support for the views you express. This support may take the form of a well-worked-out argument for holding a particular point of view. Such an argument should show in a logical way that if the reader believes certain things it follows that he should believe the conclusion that you wish to put forward. Or it may come in the form of references to the work of others; for example, you may refer to research findings they cite or arguments they employ. In Part 3 we will discuss different ways in which it is possible to support a point of view by developing an argument and also some illicit ways of persuading others to believe in a point of view. For the moment, let us say a little about referring to the work of others.

You may refer to another person's work for several reasons: because it has influenced your own thinking, because she has written something that agrees with your point of view or because she has written something that disagrees with your thoughts. These are all legitimate reasons for referring to the work of others. You should not refer to others simply to show how much you have read; if you do so you are in danger of drifting away from what is essential.

Another danger is that you may be tempted to present ideas that you do not fully understand because some writer whose name you wish to mention uses them. Whenever you use another writer's ideas you are responsible for showing not only that you understand them, but also that (and how) they are relevant to your topic. You should not assume that because some eminent thinker or writer agrees with you that this demonstrates how right you are. The fact that another author (even an eminent one) has used an idea or offered an argument does not make that idea coherent or that argument correct; there may be other equally notable writers who take an opposing point of view. In using the ideas and arguments of others to support your own point of view, you will often have to give reasons for accepting them.

Remember that it is possible to use the arguments of others in arguing in favour of your own point of view even when they disagree with you. One particularly worthwhile way of using the arguments of others, when you believe them to be inadequate, is to present them as favourably as possible and then demonstrate what is inadequate about them. This is often more impressive than simply attacking another person's arguments without explanation or adopting them because she goes along with the position you wish to support.

One very odd question that we are frequently asked by students is whether it is necessary to have a very extensive bibliography at the end of a piece of work. This question is odd because it implies that students have been given the impression by at least some lecturers that referring to other work is in some sense worthy in itself. You should only refer to another person's work if it has actually influenced your own or if by doing so you can make points that help you to build up a case. Referring to other people's work is a vacuous exercise if you do it for no other reason than to impress others with how much you have read.

## Writing references clearly

It is important whenever you cite others, to make available sufficient information to allow your reader to look up such work for herself. In order to convey bibliographical information efficiently it is best to use a system which is both easy for you to administer and easy for your reader to use. You will probably be given some instruction, however vague, about how you are expected to cite references, by your institution.

Two main systems of citation are in use. The first, the 'author-date system', is often referred to as the 'Harvard system'; the second may be referred to as the 'numeric system'. We will say a little about the method of citation in the text using each method and then about where references should be located and arranged in both systems.

## Citation using the 'Harvard system'

The Harvard system is probably the one which is most commonly used nowadays particularly in the sciences and social sciences. At every point in the text at which reference is made to a book, article or other source, the name of its author and the year of publication are inserted; full references are usually given in an alphabetical list at the end of the book, article, chapter or document. Where the author's name occurs naturally in the text, the year is given in brackets; where the author's name does not occur naturally in the text both name and date are given in brackets. If the author has published more than one work in the same year to which reference is made these are distinguished by adding lower-case letters (a, b, c etc.) after the year and inside the brackets. Where there are two authors the surnames of both are given; where there are more than two authors the surname of the first author is given, followed by '*et al.*'. In the case of anonymous works 'Anon.' is used in place of the author's name. In the case of corporate authors such as the Department of Education and Science, the appropriate abbreviation is used, in this case, DES.

*Examples*

. . . as Winch (1983) has argued . . .

. . . as many studies have suggested (e.g. Wootton 1974; Tizard and Hughes 1984; Wells 1987)

In his first article on this subject Davis (1977a) argued that . . .

In a further article (Davis 1977b) he drew attention to . . .

MacMinn and Tavistock (1963) wrote about this problem . . .

A recent study in this area (MacMinn *et al.* 1988) describes . . .

One writer (Anon. 1903) even argued that . . .

See, for example, *English in the National Curriculum* (DES, Welsh Office 1990)

If you are quoting the actual words used by another person, if the point to which you are referring may be difficult to locate, or if you are referring to different parts of a document, the appropriate page numbers may be given after the author's name and year of publication, within the brackets. For example:

In this classic study, Little (1947b, p. 25) demonstrated that . . .

For all its convenience and ease of use the Harvard system does disrupt the flow of the text and you should avoid citation except where there is a genuine need to cite support or evidence for the views you are expressing. Do not throw in textual references just to show off how much you have read or are aware of.

## Citation using the 'numeric system' of citation

The second, probably less used, system of citation may be referred to as the 'numeric system'. In this system references are indicated in the text by a superscript numeral or a numeral in parentheses at the appropriate place and full references are given either at the end of the book, article, chapter or other document, or sometimes at the foot of the page on which the citation is made. For example:

> In a recent study, Jones[1] has shown that . . .

> In a recent study, Jones (1) has shown that . . .

As with the Harvard system, if you are quoting the actual words used by another person, if the point to which you are referring may be difficult to locate, or if you are referring to different parts of a document, the appropriate page numbers may be given after the reference number in the text.

The numeric system is often combined with the use of footnotes in which an author may make an explanatory aside which is not strictly essential to the main drift of her case, perhaps supplying additional information or anticipating an objection to something she has said. Footnotes are indicated in the same way as cited work – by superscript or bracketed numerals, and are given with full references.

## Arrangement of information in bibliographical references

Where possible you should take the data for a reference directly from the cited source. A full reference should give as much information as is necessary for a reader to locate the source referred to.

The form that references should take is the same in both the Harvard and numeric systems.

### *Books*

> Surname, initials (date). <u>title</u>. place of publication, publisher.

For example, in the case of a written book:

> Fisher, A. (1988). <u>The Logic of Real Arguments</u>. Cambridge, Cambridge University Press.

and in the case of an edited book:

> Fairbairn, S. A. and Fairbairn, G. J. (eds) (1987). <u>Psychology, Ethics and Change</u>. London, Routledge & Kegan Paul.

### *Journal articles*

> Surname, initials (date). 'title of article'. <u>name of journal</u>, volume (part), pages.

For example:

> Chandler, P., Robinson, W. P. and Hoyes, P. (1988). 'The level of linguistic knowledge and awareness amongst students training to be primary teachers'. Language and Education, 2 (3), 161–74.

## *Chapters in edited books or articles reprinted in readers*

> Surname, initials (date). 'title of article or chapter'. In name of editor, initials (ed.), (date, if different from date of article) title of book. place of publication, publisher.

For example:

> Labov, W. (1969). 'The logic of non-standard English'. In Giglioli, P. (ed.), Language and Social Context. Harmondsworth, Penguin.

## *Higher degree theses and dissertations*

Higher degree theses and dissertations are handled very much like books and unpublished conference papers are handled very much like journal articles. For example:

> Fairbairn, G. J. (1980) Morality, Intention and the Development of Moral Persons. Unpublished M.Ed. dissertation, University of Manchester.

> Winch, C. A. (1981) The Theory of Restricted and Elaborated Codes: A philosophical description and evaluation of the sociolinguistic thesis of Basil Bernstein. Unpublished Ph.D. Thesis, University of Bradford.

Note that though in these examples we have used the punctuation style that we prefer for citation, there are other styles that are just as acceptable; indeed your lecturers may ask you to adopt a different style of punctuation. You will not have to look too closely to spot the difference between the punctuation we suggest here and the style in which the Open University Press has punctuated the references we cite ourselves. What is important however, is not how entries in a bibliography are punctuated, but their content. Whatever punctuation you use you should give as much information as possible and the advice we give is fairly standard nowadays about what bibliographical references should contain, though in older books you will often find less information being given.

# Location of bibliographical references

In the *Harvard system of citation* full references to all work cited are gathered in a list which usually appears at the end of the book, article or other document. References are given in strict alphabetical order of surnames; alphabetically within surnames where two or more authors you refer to have the same surname; by year of publication or letter, within individual author's work if you refer to more than one item they have published.

*Examples:*

Bandura, A. (1977) Social Learning Theory, London, Prentice-Hall.

Becker, E. (1980) The Birth and Death of Meaning (2nd Edn), Harmondsworth, Penguin.

Becker, H. S. (1968). 'The self and adult socialization'. In Norbeck, E., Price-Williams, D. and McCord, W. M. (eds) (1980). The Study of Personality. New York, Holt, Rinehart & Winston.

Ledermann, E. K. (1985a). Mental Health and Human Conscience: the True and the False Self. Aylesbury, Gower.

Ledermann, E. K. (1985b). 'Mechanism and holism in physical medicine', Explorations in Medicine, 1 (1).

Orbach, S. (1980). Fat is a Feminist Issue. London, Hamlyn.

Orbach, S. (1984). Fat is a Feminist Issue 2. London, Arrow Books.

In the *numeric system of citation* full references are given in numerical order at the end of the text or, sometimes, at the foot of the page in which the citation appears; the form adopted is the same as in the Harvard system as described above.

## Citing other sources

In this short guide to citation we have not covered all possible sources to which you may wish to refer. For example, at times you may wish to refer to other sources, for example, to film, video, radio, newspaper reports, Laws, Acts of Parliament, Government Reports, published speeches, or to personal communications which have influenced the way you think. In citing these you should follow the guidance given above for the citation within your text. Then you should deal with this reference in the same way as any other by giving as much information as you can in the appropriate place including the name of the individual to whom or the body to which you are referring, the date and place of publication or (in the case of personal communication) the date on which the conversation took place.

## Preparing bibliographies and reference lists

Keeping an up-to-date bibliographical box file will enormously assist you in preparing bibliographies for essays, allowing you to make citations easily. An alternative to the box file is to use a word processor for keeping a record of works you have consulted along with their full details. When you come to write your text on to disc you will be able to copy the references you want into the bibliography in question. Among other things this will allow you to arrange items in a bibliography, in alphabetical order without too much difficulty. It is very easy (and very frustrating) to make mistakes at this stage but a word processor will help you to overcome such mistakes without any serious problems.

## The use of direct quotation

Finally, some remarks about the use of direct quotation. At times we find that students quote rather a lot from books and articles they have read and some students even quote every time they wish to refer to another writer. This suggests a misunderstanding of the use and purpose of citation. In citing a person you may choose to cite her words directly if you could not put it better yourself. Alternatively you may quote another person's words directly if you want to be critical of her use of these particular words and it is important to let your readers know just which words you wish to object to. However, in most circumstances you need not use a person's own words in citing her.

If you do choose to cite another person's words directly you should give as precise a location for them as possible. In general if you are citing less than about 20–25 words you should incorporate the quotation within your text using quotation marks to indicate that these words belong to someone else. For quotations longer than this it is usually best to begin a new line and indent the quoted passage slightly; in this case the use of quotation marks is not usually necessary.

# 2.11  Commitment in writing

One of the themes of this book is the need to be able to communicate effectively with a readership. A second theme, no less important, is the need to respect the rationality of your readers and to seek to persuade them through evidence and argument rather than by simple assertion. (Part 3 goes into more detail on these matters.) This does not mean that as a writer you have to give up your own point of view. It is a characteristic of successful persuasive writing that the author should be *committed* to what she is writing and that she should *show* that commitment to her readers. In Section 2.2 we discussed some of the different tasks that students may be given in terms of a hierarchy of involvement or commitment. We argued that even those tasks that seem to require nothing more than description of an event or state of affairs, or of the views of another person or persons will require more than pure description; in addition they require that the student select what material to present out of a range of alternatives. Even simple description, we contend, involves commitment because it involves committing oneself to the idea that what one chooses to say about a topic is important.

This means at a minimum, that in all writing tasks in which a student engages, he should expressly commit himself to a particular point of view and seek to persuade his readership of that point of view. This may seem obvious to some of our readers but it is by no means obvious to everyone who will read this book, including lecturers as well as students. In our experience some lecturers actually discourage commitment on the part of students, requiring instead that they present a balanced and neutral (even bland) account of various positions. It is sometimes wrongly assumed that a genuine scholar will hold himself aloof from a debate, seeking only to describe the various positions on offer and the arguments for and against them. To go beyond merely stating various viewpoints in a dispassionate way is sometimes seen as an abdication of intellectual responsibility, at least while the student is an intellectual journeyman rather than a fully fledged scholar.

We strongly dissent from this view. It is of course a sign of competence when someone writing academically is able to describe and to handle the arguments in his field of study and area of controversy. But this does not, and should not, preclude him from being committed to a position whether this is one he has described that derives from others, or one that is completely different. What he does have a responsibility for is the presentation of evidence and/or rational arguments for the point of view that he holds himself and of which he is trying to persuade his readers. The writer who has something to say and something to persuade his readers of is a more interesting writer than one who is merely competent at rehearsing other people's arguments. This is as true of the undergraduate as it is of the scholar with an international reputation.

But there is even more to the matter than interesting your readers, important though that is. Commitment injects tension into the process of writing. It forces the author to engage more fully with the positions he is adopting, opposing or describing. By stating these positions fairly, he can then put them to work in order to bring out the strengths of his own case, for example, by contrasting the strength of his own position with the weakness of one he is opposing. Such an exercise tends to impose a structure on his writing that engages the reader and carries him along. An author may state his own point of view and then rehearse arguments for and against that point of view in order to give a fair run to the view he wishes eventually to reject. He may then conclude by rehearsing the arguments and stating the reasons and/or evidence for his own point of view. This strategy is sometimes known as a *dialectic,* after the argumentative character of the Socratic dialogues of Plato which are some of the most famous philosophical writings ever written. In these dialogues the tension is maintained dramatically, to a large degree through the representation of disagreement between real characters. But it is also maintained through the desire of the reader to see which position is the author's and how it will eventually emerge from the disagreements represented in the dialogue. You may care to look at some modern-day 'Socratic' dialogues contained in a book called *Philosophy in the Open* by Godfrey Vesey (1974).

We are not suggesting that you write in dialogue (although it is an interesting exercise to try and one that we have used with students), but that you try to create tension in your writing by committing yourself to a particular stance. By doing this you will become more involved with your own work. The need to understand and defend certain positions is a valuable intellectual discipline and the overall effect will be a tendency for you to develop a vigorous style which will express your commitments. With practice, you will develop a characteristic 'voice' of your own, that is, a way of setting out positions and arguing for and against them; you will cease to be the mouthpiece of other points of view and gradually become instead the articulator of your own. Remember that in speech your voice, your gestures and your facial expressions are all manifest to your audience in an immediate and obvious way, and so therefore is your commitment to what you are saying. Since you cannot use these when writing, you must make up for this by developing an individual style. That style will arise partly from your engagement with the views of others and partly from the adoption and defence of your own points of view.

One final point about commitment. Sometimes students faced with a difficult question argue that it is impossible to come up with an answer because there are competing options which they find impossible to choose between. Sometimes they find it difficult to come up with an answer because to some extent the answer will depend upon the precise meaning of the question. If you frequently find yourself having difficulty adopting a committed position in your essay writing we suggest that you ask yourself the following question: 'Is there an answer to this question?' If your answer is something like 'Well, it really depends upon what is meant by . . .' we suggest that you acknowledge that this in itself is a definite answer. Paradoxical though it may sound, it is perfectly acceptable to argue that it is impossible to give a definite answer because there is some ambiguity in the question. Recently, for example, one of us received a student essay in answer to the question 'Are children responsible?' which began 'Whether children are responsible or not depends partly upon the age or developmental stage of the children in question, partly upon their background and experience, and partly upon what we take "responsible" to mean'. The essay then went on to discuss arguments in favour of the idea that the age and background of a child affects the extent to which she is responsible and to argue in favour of a reading of the question which took 'responsible' to be referring to the capacity of children to act in a responsible fashion.

When you find difficulty in committing yourself to a particular answer it is likely that, as in this case, part of what your lecturer is looking for is a discussion of the factors that will affect the answer given: in this case a discussion of the meaning of 'responsibility' and about the differences in children at different developmental stages.

# 2.12  Finding a way of communicating

In Part 3 we will be discussing the importance of clear thinking and offering some advice about ways of developing and presenting arguments. For the moment we want to discuss the importance of style in making oneself clear in writing. The word 'style' is used in many different contexts. For example, we may say of a person that she has a 'sense of style' because we recognize that she dresses well. Writers on wine often use the word 'style' as a kind of shorthand in describing some characteristics of a wine. And of course, we talk of 'life styles', 'hair styles' and 'musical styles'.

In referring to 'style' in writing, we mean the way in which we try to communicate a message to an audience. Everyone who communicates has a style whether she is aware of it or not. In this section we want to offer some advice about ways in which you can develop your style in order to make your writing as clear, attractive and easy to read as possible.

In Part 1 and in Section 2.3 we discussed the importance of attending to the audience for whom one is writing and also to the reason one has for writing. A businessman would convey the same piece of information to his mother and to a colleague in different styles and the way we write stories for our children is different from the way in which we write for academic journals or in handouts for students. The importance of a readership in determining not only what you write but also how you write, the style you adopt, means that it is helpful to get into the habit of asking yourself 'Why am I writing this?' and 'Who am I writing it for?' whenever you sit with pen in hand or facing a word processor or typewriter.

So writing successfully involves having both a clearly thought out purpose and a clear and accurate picture of the audience for whom you are writing. As well as thinking about these things it is also necessary that you get clear about the particular points that you wish to make and attend to the structure of your written work. The way in which an author structures her writing, including the way in which she punctuates it, the order in which she presents her ideas and the relationships she makes between them, is just as important a part of her style of writing as are the words and phrases she uses. Structure has been dealt with in some detail in Section 2.4. We want now to attend to the choice of language to express ideas.

## Developing a clear and effective style of writing

Complex sentences may sound very grand but do not necessarily lead to clarity, nor does the use of pompous vocabulary or jargon. In general it is best to be as simple as is consistent with making the point you wish to make. It is better, for example, to use single words and simple phrases rather than circumlocutory ways of saying things.

Try to be direct. Get to the point quickly and clearly. Don't go round the houses making excuses for what you are not going to do or for what you have missed out or been unable to do. Don't spend lines, or worse still paragraphs, saying what you're going to do; best to get right into it! We are not suggesting that it is wrong to introduce your subject matter by giving an overview or a map of the ground you intend to cover. This can be helpful at times. However, it is often best just to get straight to the point of your essay, avoiding the possibility of beating about the bush with introductory sentences of this kind 'In order to begin to answer this question it is first necessary to consider in detail exactly what is meant by . . .'. Essays that begin like this may then do something useful in clearing the ground but too often they spend valuable words doing something that is only marginally relevant to the task. This is even more true in the case of essays that begin 'Before attempting to answer this question we must first consider . . .'. Often essays that begin like this give the impression that the student is avoiding answering the question. In general if it is necessary to discuss the meanings of words, this is better done as an integrated part of the essay rather than as an overture before the main event. Though the answer you give to a question will sometimes depend on precisely what the question means, you should utilize this fact as an aid in structuring your essay. For example, a student recently submitted an essay on the topic 'Is a child who always obeys her teachers necessarily more responsible than one who does not?' He began, 'Whether a child who always obeys her teachers is more responsible than one who does not depends on a number of factors including, for example, what is meant by "responsible". If we are talking about . . .'. Beginning his answer in this way was more direct, subtle and interesting and more focused on the question, than it would have been had he begun by writing 'Before beginning to attempt to answer this question we must first of all consider what might be meant by it'.

Another good way of introducing a topic is to 'slide up on it' sideways, as it were, rather than by approaching it head-on. This can be a way of interesting your audience before letting them know precisely what you intend to discuss. For example, one of our students, writing an essay on

'Authority and the Teacher' began with the sentence 'Some people seem to possess an ability to get other people to obey them without using force, and without giving reasons' (Wynne 1985). He then went on to discuss various different kinds of authority a teacher might possess. Another way of introducing a topic, whether at the beginning of a piece of writing or midway through it, is to offer an example that illustrates some of the points you wish to make and then discuss them. For example, H. L. A. Hart (1969) introduces the idea that there are different varieties of responsibility by relating a story about a sea captain who has certain responsibilities and fails or succeeds in fulfilling a number of them when his ship is hit by a storm. He writes:

> The following simple story of a drunken sea captain who lost his ship at sea can be told in the terminology of responsibility to illustrate, with stylistically horrible clarity, these differences of sense.
> 'As captain of the ship, X was responsible for the safety of his passengers and crew. But on his last voyage he got drunk every night and was responsible for the loss of the ship with all aboard. It was rumoured that he was insane, but the doctors considered that he was responsible for his actions. Throughout the voyage he behaved quite irresponsibly, and various incidents in his career showed that he was not a responsible person. He always maintained that the exceptional winter storms were responsible for the loss of the ship, but in the legal proceedings brought against him he was found criminally responsible for his negligent conduct, and in separate civil proceedings he was held legally responsible for the loss of life and property. He is still alive and he is morally responsible for the deaths of many women and children.'
>
> (p. 211)

As Hart himself recognizes, this story is rather unsubtle in the way it introduces the varieties of responsibility he wishes to discuss. As another example, consider further the student essay referred to above. After some introductory remarks about different kinds of authority the student illustrated these with the following story:

> Consider the situation of a road traffic accident. Someone, often a passer-by, comes on the scene and delegates instructions which people follow immediately – 'Go and ring for an ambulance', or 'Fetch a blanket'. Any observers of the accident may have been stunned and are unsure what to do. The 'charismatic' authority which the stranger brings to the situation inspires people to act, they are acting 'on the authority' of the stranger. If a policeman had come onto the scene and given instructions he would be representing 'traditional' authority, the person 'in-authority' at the roadside. However, the stranger may be insane, not knowing what he is saying, a person who walks the streets shouting the same instructions every day of his life, he could even be wearing a uniform similar to the uniform of the St John Ambulance

Brigade. Due to the fact that the observers do not know this man personally, they readily accept the apparent 'rational' authority of his commands, acting on the basis that the stranger is 'an authority'. In this example the observers have followed the instructions given, but the 'authority' which they have accepted for the basis of their actions could have been any of the types of authority which Young and Weber offer. The form of authority in this example hinges on two factors, the true status of the stranger, and the observers' view of the stranger.

(Paul Wynne 1985)

In this way the student introduced some of the points he wanted to make about different varieties of authority, through a memorable example.

The more adequate the language we use to convey what we are thinking when we write, the more likely it is that our reader will be able to understand what we wish her to understand. It is therefore important to think carefully about the words we use. In Sections 2.13 and 2.14 we will discuss the choice of language. We want now to discuss a particularly important aspect of style: whether one should write in the first or rather the third, person.

# 2.13 First, second or third person?

Very young writers tend to express themselves most naturally from a point of view that is both informal and personal. They address the reader in a familiar way, inviting her to take part in their point of view, most often adopting the grammatical idiom known as 'first person' which is characterized by the use of the pronouns 'I' and 'we'. For example, 'I went to the theatre yesterday' or 'We are going on holiday at the weekend'. In other words, the young writer invites you to see the world from his point of view and is not backward about sharing his opinions with you. With luck (and good teaching) as he matures, he will learn to master different kinds of writing and to understand and use the different levels of formality that are appropriate to different styles of writing. By early adolescence the student should be able to write in an *impersonal* style, not allowing his personality to intrude into the text or bringing himself directly to the attention of the reader; he should be able to use a style of writing that does not display his own (or indeed, anyone else's) special point of view. At this stage he will be able to write in the grammatical idiom known as the 'third person' which is characterized by the presence of the third person pronouns 'it', 'he', 'they' and so on, in the subject. He will probably, also, be able to write in the 'second person' where the writer directly addresses the reader. Thus, for example, 'Choose language that is as simple as is compatible with what you wish to communicate' is written in the second person. Writing in the second person can have an intimacy, an immediacy about it that is absent from a more formal, third person style. Throughout this book, when we give direct advice, we normally use the second person in an effort to engage our readers.

Impersonal writing is more difficult to master than personal writing and is often used in academic work for reasons which we will discuss presently. Students are often given the impression that impersonal writing is somehow superior to other more personal forms of address. Though this is not true, an impersonal style is very often appropriate when the writer's opinions, experiences and perspective are not strictly relevant to the material being discussed in, say, a descriptive essay or report. Youngsters find this impersonal mode of address the most difficult to master and many adult writers also find it unfamiliar and at times difficult to handle.

Examples of occasions when impersonal writing is appropriate include scientific reports, technical manuals, reports for insurance companies, and recipes in cookery books. Much of the writing that may be expected of you as a student will fall into this category. For example, if you are required to write a review of literature or to discuss the implications of results or data as part of a piece of writing in the social sciences, you will probably be expected to adopt the third person. In the physical sciences it is even more likely that you will be expected to write in the third person. For example, if you are required to give an account of an experiment in a chemistry laboratory or to describe the mineral content of a thin section of rock in a geology laboratory you will most likely be expected to adopt this style: 'When the two solutions were mixed together the following changes were noted to occur . . .' or 'The pyroxene crystals were observed to change colour as the thin section was rotated in polarized light'. In most scientific contexts the use of the first person is considered inappropriate. So, for example, you would not write: 'I loved the bit in the experiment where we mixed the two solutions together and everything started to happen' or 'The sight of the pyroxene crystals changing colour as I rotated the section in polarized light really knocked me out'. You may notice that these cases are not simply examples of the use of the first person; in addition they are colloquial in character. However, even a more formal use of the first person is generally unacceptable in physical science. So, although it would be less colloquial to write: 'When the two solutions were mixed together I noted the following colour changes . . .' and 'I observed the pyroxene crystals changing colour as the thin section was rotated in polarized light', even such uses of the first person would probably still be considered unusual.

The most common way of distinguishing between writing that is personal in style and writing that is impersonal, is that whereas personal writing most often utilizes the first person, impersonal writing is most often third person in character. It is important to note, however, that a third person style need not imply a lack of commitment on the part of the writer; nor need it be dry or impersonal in the sense that the reader has no sense of the presence of the writer. Conversely, the use of the first person need not mean that the writer intends to do nothing more than talk about herself; it is possible to use the first person in writing, for example, about abstract ideas. It is also important to realize that experienced writers often switch between the first and third person throughout the course of a piece of writing.

We do not intend to go into a detailed discussion of the differences between first, second and third person writing. Rather, let us give some examples of each.

*First person writing*

(i)   I was going down the road when I heard a loud noise that really made me jump. I was very scared at first but when I realized that it was only a cat knocking over a dustbin, I began to relax a little.

(ii)  I would argue that third person writing, far from being the style most appropriate for academic writing, is singularly unsuited to it.

*Second person writing*

(i)   You should attend carefully to the words you use. In particular, ensure that you do not use words with which you are unfamiliar.

(ii)  You may think the third person is more appropriate than the first person, for academic writing. On the other hand, you may not share this very common view, believing it to be outmoded and rather pompous.

*Third person writing*

(i)   It is possible to argue that the third person is more appropriate for academic writing.

(ii)  The cement was mixed with sand and water in the proportions suggested; the resulting mixture became quite hard in twenty-four hours.

The requirements of some forms of academic writing will often indicate that the third person is most appropriate or at any rate expected. Thus for example, whereas it would make perfect sense and would not be intrusively personal, to write 'I monitored the colour change carefully' in scientific writing it would be usual to write 'The colour change was carefully monitored'. Even in situations where the first person would in no way detract from, or alter the sense intended, it is often conventional to write in the third person; in scientific papers and reports the convention of writing in the third person is so well established that to do anything else is likely to be frowned upon.

However, it will sometimes be equally appropriate to write in the first person. There may even be occasions where the first person will be much more appropriate: for example, when the writer wishes to make her presence felt in the text by giving her own opinion or referring to an event in her experience.

The over-frequent use of 'I' can have the effect of bringing the writer too obtrusively into the picture. So even where you are writing in the first person, you should avoid the excessive use of the personal pronoun 'I' both for the sake of elegance and in order to avoid the danger that your writing becomes little more than an account of your unworked feelings, thoughts, opinions and experiences. Unless you are writing an autobiographical account, your audience is unlikely to be interested in your personal experience. Personal experience may inform your writing and thinking; but you should take care to avoid lapsing into anecdote; the danger of doing so is probably the principal reason for the somewhat unconsidered exhortations of many of those who demand third person writing. It is almost always advisable to avoid chattiness in academic writing whether at the student or the professional level. One particularly bad mistake that students sometimes make is when they put jokes into an essay; this is inadvisable unless the joke in question is unusually appropriate and helps to make a serious point. It is more likely that the reader is going to resent such informality on the part of the author as an intrusive diversion from concentrating on what she has to say and to feel that the *bonhomie* is at best forced or at worst patronizing.

## Should you adopt first or third person?

To some extent whether you write in the first or third person as a student is a matter of personal preference. However, to some extent it may be dictated by the requirements of your course or those who teach you; students are often told to use the third person when writing essays. Though we think that this expectation may result in worse essays, it is as well to pay attention to what is expected of you.

It could be very appropriate to write in the first person in a literary, theological or philosophical essay. By writing in the first person one owns the opinions and views one presents; this could be appropriate for these disciplines. However, it is less likely to be appropriate to write in the first person in an essay written in a pure science discipline. The adoption of the less personal and more distant stance which is characteristic of much third person writing is, as we have said, conventional in contexts such as science, where objectivity is seen as important. In general it is best to obey conventions that apply to the arena in which you are writing.

It is important that you realize that first and third person writing may readily be translated one into the other. Thus the sentence 'It seems to me that this argument is mistaken' may be translated as the third person sentence 'This argument seems to be mistaken'. And whereas in the first person you might write 'I would argue that . . .' in the third person you would write 'It might be argued that . . .'

Some of the ugliest writing we have come across involves the use of what looks like the third person when what is written amounts to no more than a poor translation from first into third person language. The frequently used expressions 'In the opinion of the present author . . .' or 'The writer of this essay . . .' are ugly because they use too many words and they are still essentially first person in style though pretending to be something else. How much more simple to write 'In my opinion . . .' or 'I . . .'.

When the third person is used in this way it can look and sound awful, conveying an impression of pomposity. Writing 'In the opinion of the present author . . .' or 'The writer considers that . . .' instead of 'It is my opinion that . . .' or 'I consider that . . .' is usually no more than an affectation of style. Often students will use euphemisms of this kind throughout an essay.

However, there are occasions where it can be helpful to use expressions such as 'the present author' sparingly. An example may be where you are writing in the third person and wish to draw on your personal experience in such a way that you do not sound boastful or overbearing. The use of 'the present author/writer' can also serve to keep the author from sounding as if he is claiming an authoritative position on the basis of his personal experience which he is not really entitled to claim. Consider, for example, the following passage:

> How different is the experience at primary school of girls from boys?
> In the present writer's professional experience, there is no obvious difference between boys and girls in achievement except perhaps in favour of the latter.
>
> (Winch 1985)

This extract is taken from what, in the main, is a piece of third person writing. In talking about the author's experience, 'The present writer' is consciously used to avoid jarring of style. This is different from the use to which we have referred above.

Writing in the third person has other hazards apart from the possibility that when used badly it can convey an impression of pomposity. For example, it can at times convey an impression of bureaucratic insensitivity which is quite unnecessary. Here is a memo by which a member of staff learned that she was about to be thrown out of her room. It is not difficult to think of ways of doing this better; perhaps you would like to try. Notice that the memo, though directed to G. Pugh, is intended also to convey to Dr Jones that her office is to be relocated.

From:  Dr J. L. Evans
To:     Dr G. Pugh
c.c.    Dr F Jones

Centre for the Study of Human Relationships – Room Location

It is the wish of the Dean of Human Relationships to associate Dr Jones more closely with the Centre for the Study of Human Relationships and, in this context, would like her tutorial base to be physically located within the Centre. It is understood that her present location is under review because of alterations to her current accommodation and this would seem an appropriate time to make such a move.

It is anticipated that this will cause problems and may involve some refurbishment/alteration etc., to the existing accommodation but he is anxious that the move should happen and not be inhibited by the difficulties mentioned. It may be possible to 'fund' some internal room alterations and you are asked to examine the best outcome in consultation with Dr Evans but the move should be a priority in early Autumn notwithstanding the possible absence of any resource help.

Readers may wish to note Dr Evans's apparent inability to construct sentences in grammatical English as well as his unwillingness to use the English language in a stylistically clear manner. It is passive, long winded nonsense and does not serve its purpose well (these things are discussed later when we come to discuss gobbledegook and pomposity).

## Writing well in the first person

It is possible to write well in the first person, to address the reader person-to-person, and yet avoid lapsing into what amounts to no more than a telling of part of the story of one's life to date. For example, in an entertaining paper entitled 'Psychologists Are Human Too' in which he addresses the tendency of psychologists to detach themselves from their subjects, Mair (1970) began:

> When I hear people accuse psychologists of being isolated from the real world, small minded, hidebound by doctrine and method, incapable of learning from experience, I have to laugh. After all, I know, personally, half a dozen (well at least three) psychologists who, after only a few years of dedicated experimentation in their discipline, and despite very expensive and lengthy training to the contrary, have been forced to change some of their fundamental professional beliefs and accept that the subjects they have been herding through their laboratories *are human* after all.

In this short passage Mair manages, in a personal and witty style, both to engage his readership and to give them a good idea of what is to come. In addition, since it is his intention to criticize psychologists' habit of attempting to remain aloof and distant from their subjects, almost as if they can pursue research in a totally objective and impersonal way, it is fitting that he should write in a personal style.

# Writing well in the third person

Just as first person writing need not be too personal in the sense that it involves simply giving an account of part of one's life to date, one's personal experiences and so on, so third person writing need not be impersonal, distant and uninvolved, although this will often be appropriate. The writer may wish to stay out of the picture as an individual, but this does not prevent her from writing with a sense of involvement. This can be achieved while at the same time focusing the reader on, for example, a description, without excessively directing the attention of the reader to the author. Consider, for example, the following extract from an article by A. S. Byatt in the *Independent Magazine*:

> Nimes is a civilised town. It lies in the sun, its ancient Roman monuments, its beautiful formal garden, the Jardin de la Fontaine, built in the 18th century by a military engineer, its narrow cobbled streets and wide boulevards, its elegant shops and solidly civilised old houses, all part of one harmonious whole. Its name derives from a spring, guarded by a divinity named Nemausus. Augustus Caesar gave this land to the veterans of his victorious Egyptian campaign against Antony and Cleopatra. They must have lived there in a sunny abundance quite different from the wind whistling chill in my North, celebrated by Kipling and W. H. Auden. The city's symbol is still the chained crocodile of the Nile who often appears in various witty forms, often accompanied by a palm tree. He is there on the street drain-covers, he is picked out in flowers in the Jardin de la Fontaine, he is sculpted in bronze in the Place du Marché, where he lies on the side of the fountain, within reach of a real palm tree.
>
> (A. S. Byatt, *Independent Magazine* 3 March 1990, p. 41)

In this extract, though Byatt is writing in the third person, she is very much present because of the content of what she is writing about, which gives us as readers a sense that we are looking over her shoulder as she walks round this grand old city.

We took a deliberate decision to write predominantly in the first person in this book, though as a glance through the book will demonstrate we do not avoid either the third or the second person. Indeed, as we have said, we have chosen to use the second person when we are offering advice.

# Picking and mixing

It is possible to write in a way that incorporates both first and third person forms and yet to be quite coherent. For example, at the beginning of his famous book *A Theory of Justice* (1971), the philosopher John Rawls is discussing the role of justice in social institutions. Referring to some remarks he has made about just societies he writes:

> These propositions seem to express our intuitive conviction of the primacy of justice. No doubt they are expressed too strongly. In any event I wish to inquire whether these contentions or others similar to them are sound, and if so how they can be accounted for. To this end it is necessary to work out a theory of justice in the light of which these assertions can be interpreted and assessed. I shall begin by considering the role of the principles of justice. Let us assume, to fix ideas, that a society is . . .
>
> (p. 4)

In this passage Rawls switches between first and third person as it suits him. At times he is giving an account of what he, John Rawls, believes or intends to do; at others he is making general remarks about his subject matter.

Or consider the following passage from the beginning of an article about euthanasia and infanticide, a serious issue if ever there was one:

> Quality of life frequently figures in discussions about life and death: about, for example, whether a life is likely to be of such poor quality that it can be justifiable (even merciful) to deny its bearer treatment that will prolong it. I propose to contrast the importance which quality of life is given in such situations, which occur mostly at the beginning of life, with the importance it may be given at the end of life.
>
> (Fairbairn 1991)

In this paragraph the author introduces his topic using the third person but moves into the first person when he announces the particular issue he intends to address.

# 2.14  Choosing the right words

Words are the tools with which you make meaning and the better suited to the job the tools you use, the more likely you are to succeed in conveying your ideas clearly. You should therefore take great care in choosing words when you write.

## Using words appropriately

Not only must you choose the best words, you must also ensure that you use words appropriately. Using short, everyday words will often be more effective than using more difficult ones; in general therefore, they are to be preferred unless longer words help to convey your meaning more clearly. We are not suggesting that there is anything wrong with the longer words of the English language; we are merely pointing out that they are often misused and even abused by writers whose desire to impress people with their cleverness is stronger than their desire to communicate clearly.

You should not use words and phrases whose meanings you are unclear about, without extreme caution. Never use a word that you do not really understand in the hope that your reader will be impressed because it is long or impressive sounding.

Whenever you feel tempted to abandon a familiar word for a more impressive sounding one, ask yourself whether you need the particular meaning the less common word conveys. If you are going to use a word with which you are unfamiliar, check with a dictionary or in one of your textbooks that you are going to use it accurately. Neglecting this advice can produce amusing results. For example, a student once referred to a psychological phenomenon known as the Oedipus complex, which roughly speaking is the difficult period that psychoanalytic thinkers believe that little boys go through with their fathers and during which they are particularly close to their mothers. This would have been rather impressive except that the student referred to the 'edifice complex'. This mistake made the reference less than impressive because it seems likely that the student had made a mistake in taking notes at a lecture and had failed to check out what he had noted down by reference to any other source, before writing his essay. If you want to enlarge your vocabulary and avoid repetition of particular words in expressing your ideas, *Roget's Thesaurus of English Words and Phrases* is a worthwhile resource.

Finally it is worth noting the importance of using words accurately. Sometimes people can use words that sound alike in the wrong context. Consider for example the student, writing an essay about the dangers of indoctrination for teachers who wrote the following:

> The indoctrinator on the other hand will intend to install one point of view and one point of view only . . .

This student has luckily hit upon a combination of words which almost makes sense. However, whereas it might be possible to use the word 'install' metaphorically to refer to the 'installation' of ideas in the minds of others, we feel sure that in this instance the writer intended to talk of them being instilled and had merely confused the words 'install' and 'instil'.

## Synonyms

Synonyms are words that mean the same thing, or very nearly the same thing, as one another. The English language is particularly rich in such words because modern English has emerged from a hotchpotch of various other languages. The happy result is that there will often be a choice of words which may be used with equal correctness in a given context. However, there are dangers in having a rich language available on which to draw. One of these dangers stems from the fact that synonyms are not necessarily interchangeable. Though several words may mean the same, or very nearly the same, as one another, it is often not possible to exchange one for the other in a simple way because convention as well as meaning dictates the ways in which many words are used. For example, though 'start' and 'begin' can mean something very similar to one another, you would not write 'The Judge began the race by firing a gun', you would write that he started it. Nor would you write 'Residence, sweet residence' or 'An Englishman's residence is his castle', because 'residence' does not carry the same cosy feeling as 'home'. 'Residence' is often used by estate agents in rather amusing ways. It implies something grand, as in the sentences 'The ambassador's residence was built in the Palladian style' and 'The Palace of Holyrood is the Queen's official residence in Scotland'. When estate agents use it to give an air of gentility to a description of a house for sale by, for example, referring to a two-up and two-down terraced house as 'a delightful gentleman's residence', it serves to do little more than amuse.

So you should try to avoid using words in contexts which are a bit odd for them; this is particularly important when using a word with which you are unfamiliar.

There is a pompous version of the song 'Show Me the Way to go Home' which is amusing because it uses words in ways that are rather strange. The song goes:

Show me the way to go home
I'm tired and I want to go to bed
I had a little drink about an hour ago
And it's gone right to my head
No matter where I roam
O'er land or sea or foam
You will always find me singing this song
'Show me the way to go home'

Try completing the pompous version which begins:

Indicate the way to my abode
I'm fatigued and I wish to retire
. . .

## Avoid confusing your reader

(i)   Your job is to convey meaning, not to confuse or frustrate your reader by using words with which she is unfamiliar. So not only should you avoid words that are unfamiliar to you, you should also, if possible, avoid words that you do not expect your readers to understand unless you are prepared – and able – to explain what you mean by them. You must consider carefully whether it is reasonable to expect your readers to be familiar with the words you are using. Do not assume too readily that your teachers will be familiar with specialized vocabulary unless you are sure that it is part of the general vocabulary of their discipline. This point is especially true in relation to common words that have been hijacked from everyday language and made to fulfil a particular function within a specialist area, and 'newspeak' words, that is, words that have been invented relatively recently to fulfil a particular function. Whenever you are going to use very new words, you should consider whether their use will help you to be clearer than you could be without them.

Some years ago when we taught philosophy together we had a rash of essays on the topic 'Can we teach children to be good?' by students who had clearly come across some terms coined by the philosopher John Wilson. In his book *The Assessment of Morality* (1973) Wilson proposed, among other things, that there are a number of different dimensions to morality which he labels by a series of odd words including 'dik', 'krat' and 'emp' which he derived from Greek. Neither of us has ever found this proliferation of terms particularly useful, but our students, clearly labouring under the illusion that we were all-knowing and all-understanding, and therefore expecting us to be thoroughly familiar with Wilson's terms, began using them as if they were common English words. This was a mistake partly because they were making their writing more difficult to understand than was necessary and partly because they were showing a lack of discrimination in relation to things they had read. Wilson, as we have already indicated, is a well-known philosopher and his work in relation to moral development is highly regarded by many people, but that does not necessarily mean that everything he writes is worth adopting, far less that it is in some sense generally accepted.

(ii) Language is never static. As a product of human activity it changes according to purpose, preoccupation and fashion but readers are entitled to know if a word is being used with a very recent meaning. You should use words in their usual sense unless you state that you are going to do otherwise; if you do, your usage and your reasons for using a word outside its usual sense, should be clearly stated. The use of the word 'gender' to mean 'sex' is an example of a word that is more and more frequently used outside its usual context. 'Gender' originally referred to certain properties of parts of speech. More recently, in, for example, the literature of social psychology, it has come to be used to mean something like 'socially constructed perception of sexual identity' as opposed to 'sex' which refers to one's sexual classification according to physical characteristics. Under the influence of fashion, the term 'gender' has come sometimes to be used to mean pretty much the same as what 'sex' has always meant.

Another example of this kind of change in the way in which words are used is the use of the word 'text' which is normally used to refer to a passage of writing. This expression is now sometimes used to denote practically anything that has meaning or significance. For example, someone might refer to a speech by a politician as a 'text' or to a film, exhibition of paintings, sculpture or photographs, as a text because it makes a significant statement. She may even refer to an individual person as a text, as in the statement 'Mrs Thatcher is the text for tonight's discussion'. It could be argued that to extend the use of the expression 'text' in this way is to devalue its original use to refer to written material.

(iii)  Inappropriate words do not do their job well however good they sound and you should take care to choose words that are appropriate for the audience for whom you are writing. You would not use the same language in explaining to a four-year-old your understanding of the hole in the ozone layer, as you would to a well-educated undergraduate, especially if he was a science student; nor would the amount of detail you would attempt to offer be the same in each case.

(iv)  Avoid using too many words. Choosing words carefully can help to make your writing interesting, easy to read, concise and accurate. Choosing words which convey meaning as precisely as possible helps to avoid the confusion which can result from using too many words. At best using too many words simply adds nothing; at worst it can actually obscure meaning. Do take this point seriously. We can all be guilty of longwindedness. In our first draft of this book the sentence 'Avoid using too many words' read 'One thing to avoid is the use of too many words'. Did the extra six words convey anything more?

One characteristic of longwinded writing is the use of excessively long sentences. Long sentences can make for difficult reading and poor communication. Consider, for example, the following sentence from an essay written by a student; he is discussing the place of aesthetic pursuits in the curriculum:

> We are aesthetic beings long before we are rational beings, since, from a new-born babe, a person begins to mediate his or her world through the basic senses of sight, sound, smell, touch, and taste, thus bringing together through pain, pleasure or a sense of well-being, intimations of the nature of our world, and with it, a commitment to basic understanding; the development of which demands a particular kind of imaginative attention to things made, performed or learned; and in doing so, become critically reflective in his or her responses to them.

This sentence is so long that though it gives the impression of coherence, it is difficult to hold on to its sense till one gets to the end. It has several strands and the use of semi-colons towards the end suggests that the writer is aware that there are too many separate ideas for one sentence. Try rewriting it in, say, three or four sentences to see whether this can help to make its meaning clearer.

It could, for example, be rewritten as follows:

> We are aesthetic beings long before we are rational beings. From a new-born babe, a person begins to mediate his or her world through the basic senses of sight, sound, smell, touch and taste and thus brings together through pain, pleasure or a sense of well-being, intimations of the nature of our world. Through these experiences comes a commitment to basic understanding the development of which demands a particular kind of imaginative attention to things made, performed or learned. In so doing the person becomes critically reflective in his or her responses to them.

(v)   The use of too many words can cause confusion by side-tracking your reader. Another way in which confusion can be caused is by the overuse of particular words. Consider for example, the following report of a meeting of the Rigsby Rural Society:

> The meeting had an interesting talk on jam making by Mrs Brown, who also answered many interesting questions. The results of the raffle were then received with great interest. A most interesting visit to an interesting paper doily factory is planned for next month if there is sufficient interest.

Though the members of the Rigsby Rural Society might be 'interested' in their activities the lack of 'interesting' language on the part of their secretary makes her account of their proceedings rather boring.

Or consider something that Dan Quayle said in the speech that we referred to in Section 2.4. Having thanked Him for many things Quayle went on to give thanks for the freedom 'to elect the representatives to represent them in a free, representative society' (Jehl op. cit.)

We suggest that you pay close attention to the need to avoid repetition of words, if necessary using a thesaurus to locate alternative words which allow you to be both precise and elegant. At times, though, it might prove necessary to repeat a word if you wish your meaning to be clear; ultimately it is more important to be clear than to be elegant. However, in general it is best to avoid the undue repetition of words because repetition can hinder clarity as well as being boring.

(vi)  Problems can also arise if you put together words that have some similarity in sound. We would not write that 'The Principal's principle principle was that she, as Principal, should be principally responsible for decision making', or 'Generals generally generate a lot of energy'.

Not only do these sentences sound odd, they are also difficult to read and understand because we get distracted by the rhyme and rhythm of the words.

## Jargon and technical language

'Jargon' is used to refer to the specialized vocabulary of a specific field of work or study, for example, sociology, the law, computers or economics. Within such fields the use of jargon can be justified because it can help meanings to be communicated more accurately and more briefly than by using the general vocabulary. While it is reasonable to expect people working within an academic or professional field to understand its technical language, outside that field there can be no expectation that it will be understood and so, outside the linguistic community from which it stems, it is best to avoid jargon. In a way using specialized vocabulary outside its area of legitimate operation can devalue its technical use and lead to its losing the precise meaning it has, at least when used in a casual way. If you do want to use jargon words, make sure that your readers understand the jargon or be prepared to explain it to them.

Used out of context specialized vocabulary is often used inaccurately. You should therefore use everyday terms rather than jargon, where possible. In particular you should avoid using jargon words because they sound good or because you've just read them; in using jargon words with which you are unfamiliar there is always a danger that you will make mistakes with disastrous consequences. If you find that you want to use words that you have good reason to believe have a very specific meaning within a particular field, make sure before doing so that you are using them correctly.

So jargon is acceptable only when you're writing for an audience whom you have every reason to believe will be familiar with the language in which you're writing and its use allows you to make yourself clear in a more concise way than you could without it. After all, you wouldn't write in French for an audience who didn't speak French, so why write in computerese or some other jargon for readers who don't understand computerese or this other jargon? The authors of computer manuals are probably some of the worst offenders. We won't say which word processing packages we have used in writing this book but their technical authors certainly have a thing or two to answer for.

# 2.15  Stylistic traps

In Section 2.13 we discussed the importance of care in choosing words when trying to make sense and communicate in writing. We now want,

briefly, to visit some stylistic traps that all writers are in danger of falling
into. We will call first on longwindedness, pomposity and gobbledegook
and then visit some varieties of frozen language including cliché.

## Longwindedness, pomposity and gobbledegook

Students sometimes have the misguided notion that using long words and
complex sentences will make a good impression. In general it is better to be
simple than complex, both at the level of the word and at the level of the
sentence or paragraph. Thus, as we have suggested, the use of jargon and
difficult words is to be avoided unless using them can help to make your
meaning clearer and you know that the audience will understand what a
particular word means or you explain what you are using it to mean. In a
similar way it is best to avoid long and complex sentences and to make your
style of writing as simple as is consistent with saying what you want to say.
Sometimes we read essays from students which, on a cursory glance, seem
to be written in reasonable language: they use a range of vocabulary and so
on. However, on closer examination it becomes clear that though they
obviously mean something, just what they mean is going to be difficult to
ascertain. In Part 3 we will argue in favour of approaching work written by
others with the intention of being generously critical, trying to understand
what they are saying, rather than adopting an adversarial approach in
which the object is to prove how inadequate the writer is. Even when
adopting a generous approach, however, it is at times difficult to work out
what a student intends by an essay. Often this is because the language he
uses is pompous and longwinded and seems to be attempting to sound
important and academic rather than genuinely to communicate. For
example, one of us recently read an essay which contained the following
sentence: 'The tiger which the teacher is currently riding, with a mixture of
aplomb and anxiety, is certainly not static'. This sentence appeared in an
essay addressing the question of who should decide on the curriculum of
our schools. It was difficult to work out just what the student intended by it
and having worked that out it was then necessary to work out just what was
meant by the many other similar, and often much longer and more
complex, sentences that appeared in the same essay. Simplicity and
directness are in the end the best way to be clear.

In relation to a discussion of the difference between the informal and the
loose and unscholarly, Straughan and Wilson (1983) point out that 'the
sombre and decorous trappings of scholarship need to be distinguished
from scholarship itself' (p. vi). Sounding as if one is saying something
important by using impressive sounding words and complex constructions
does not necessarily mean that one is actually doing so. It is impressive
when a piece of writing succeeds in being clear about what its writer

intended to communicate. Avoiding the unnecessary use of long words and complicated constructions will make it more likely that what you write will be successful in communicating.

The details of houses for sale prepared by estate agents are often a minefield of misuses of language. They are often complex, pompous and fanciful. We have already referred to the use they sometimes make of the word 'residence' to imply something grander than a realistic description of a small house might otherwise convey. This and many other aspects of the prose they write are intended to impress and no doubt they do impress and even mislead, some people. We doubt whether anyone who is impressed by them would write a decent essay. For example, consider the following:

> This elegant and extremely well maintained 'olde worlde' house is situated in a well established older style neighbourhood, far from the beaten track and the extensive accommodation extends to a lounge, six bedrooms, including boxroom/study, large kitchen and separate utility/pantry, fully fitted floor and wall cupboards and many other features which make this residence one that we would recommend any discerning prospective purchaser should visit without delay owing to its desirability as a family home with potential for guesthouse/rest home.

This description is longwinded and pompous. Students, like estate agents, sometimes use long and complex, often rather technical, words and constructions as a substitute for clear thinking because they think that their use will impress. This is just silly, particularly where it is obvious that the writer does not understand the vocabulary he is using. Longwindedness is to be avoided for two reasons: it can obscure meaning and it uses up words that could have been used saying something worthwhile. You should avoid using several words where one will do. So, for example, you should not write 'in many instances' if you mean 'often' and it would be better to write 'While I was studying . . .' than 'During the time that I was engaged in a study of . . .'.

Politicians frequently use longwinded constructions to buy time and give a certain weight to what they are saying. For example, rather than saying 'nevertheless' they often say 'be that as it may'. They frequently refer to 'this moment in time' when they could say 'now' or claim that they are 'now in a position to' do something rather than simply saying that they are 'now able' to do so. Sometimes they tell us that something happened 'at an earlier date' when they could have said it happened 'earlier' or 'previously'. All of those longwinded constructions turn up in student essays which shows that some students pay more attention to what politicians say in their speeches than they do to being as brief as possible.

Sometimes longwindedness is combined with a certain affectation of style to produce pomposity. Fisher Cassie and Constantine (1977) cite A. P. Herbert's suggested translation of a famous line from English history:

It is anticipated that, as regards the current emergency, personnel will face up to the issues and exercise appropriately the functions allocated to their respective age groups.

This is a somewhat pompous way of translating Nelson's signal to his men at the battle of Trafalgar:

England expects that every man will do his duty.

*Exercise*
Here are a couple of famous sayings rendered into pompous and longwinded gobbledegook. They come from Madawc Williams's 'It's only Words' in the *Labour and Trade Union Review*. no 16, March–April, 1990, p. 4. Can you work out what they are?

(i)   In the absence of the feline predator the rodent scavengers can engage in recreational activity.
(ii)  A repair implemented at this point in time will yield a net saving of human resources of the order of 88.899%.

Of course these translate as:

(i)   When the cat's away the mice will play.
(ii)  A stitch in time saves nine.

Whenever you find yourself tempted to use pompous sounding words, or longwinded expressions rather than simple, more direct ones, you are likely to be attempting to impress others with how clever you are. At these times think again, and find other words.

At times longwindedness and pomposity go even further and turn into what might be referred to as gobbledegook. Gobbledegook is an accumulation of different communication sins including the unnecessary use of big words, the use of redundant words, and what we might refer to as the 'linguistic roundabout' where a writer gets herself into a muddle by using such convoluted structures that she ends up saying nothing very much. Here is a fine example of the linguistic roundabout which is cited by Burton (1982):

In so far as they can be projected, the adverse economic factors in the immediately foreseeable future are likely to be of the order presently pertaining.

(p. 122)

This translates as:

It is unlikely that present adverse economic factors will change soon.

Burton also gives the following example of gobbledegook of a passive and impersonal kind:

It is desired to draw attention to the necessity that the regulations governing procedures established to ensure safety in the event of fire should be observed by all residents.

In other words:

> Residents should obey the fire-drill regulations.

At times gobbledegook is deliberate: the writer or speaker is attempting to confuse or mislead the listener or reader. Some of the finest examples of gobbledegook of this kind are fictional. Here, for example, is one drawn from the TV comedy series *Yes, Prime Minister*:

> Dear Prime Minister,
>
> When I said that HA was not overstretched, I was of course talking in the sense of total cumulative loading taken globally rather than in respect of certain individual and essentially anomalous responsibilities which are not, logically speaking, consonant or harmonious with the broad spectrum of intermeshing and inseparable functions and could indeed be said to place an excessive and supererogatory burden on the office when considered in relation to the comparatively exigious advantages of their overall consideration.
>
> Yours ever,
>
> Frank

This example is, of course, fictional and we need hardly point out its failings as a piece of communication. However, students and even professional academics at times write things that are very similar. For example, discussing the treatment of human embryos shortly before proposed legislation relating to embryo research came before Parliament, Nigel S. de Cameron wrote the following remarkable sentence:

> May we not argue that the way in which such conflicts should be met in our society involves (a) a cautious and conservative approach to fundamental change; (b) a recognition that certain courses of action are ruled out, since they are profoundly offensive to many people (majority? substantial minority? – so much depends on how the question is framed); (c) an awareness that there are arguments unconnected with Christian religious and ethical convictions which tend to support them, or (put it another way) to show that they are reasonable (in this case we are working with a concept of human rights and human dignity as co-extensive with Homo sapiens)?
>
> (Nigel, S. de Cameron, 'Embryos again',
> *Ethics and Medicine*, 1989, 5 (2) p. 17)

Perhaps as an exercise you may care to try writing down what you think de Cameron intends here. It seems to us that though it is clear he intends something, the convoluted nature of this sentence with its three-point list, asides and questions, makes it difficult by the end to remember what the beginning of the sentence was about.

Another way in which people sometimes try to make what they are saying sound more worthy than it actually is, is by elaborating what they say by the addition of useless words. For example, they might refer to something as being 'absolutely perfect' instead of 'perfect'. Someone trying to persuade you to take a holiday in her hilly resort might refer to it as being 'hilly in character' instead of 'hilly'; she might refer to something as being 'really impossible' instead of 'impossible' or to something as 'absolutely unique' instead of 'unique' (either a thing is unique or it isn't; there are no gradations of uniqueness).

# Frozen language

At times language can become frozen into stylized uses in which forms of words are used in rather an unthinking way. When this happens the speaker or writer has not really thought about what she is wishing to communicate but rather has simply grabbed at whatever ready-made phrases she has to hand.

The best example of frozen language is cliché. 'Cliché' is a French word; it used to refer to common words, phrases and sentences that printers kept ready to save them the bother of making up new blocks every time they needed them. 'Cliché' now refers to a common word, phrase or sentence that trips easily off the tongue. Clichés have lost their original effectiveness through overuse. Often they were once rather powerful metaphors conveying meaning in strikingly new ways until overuse made them pale and insipid, even something to be laughed at.

Consider, for example, the lecturer in a teacher training college, who, in an attempt to be (if you'll pardon the clichés) 'where it's at', 'right on' and 'hip' in his language, says things of this kind:

> What we want is bums on seats. You need street cred in this business, so those of us with pockets full of chalk dust must get down to the grass roots and ask the punters what they want. We've got to get alongside them – on the same wave length – if we're going to catch their drift. Then we've got to sock it to them. If we don't get our act together we're off down the Swannee.

Roughly translated this means something like

> We need to make sure that our recruitment is on target. We must become aware of the training needs of teachers and tailor our courses accordingly. This will involve close liaison between schools and those of us who have more recently been serving teachers. If we don't do this, we can expect this college to be closed.

Some of the worst examples of cliché are also examples of mixed metaphor. Consider, for example, the same lecturer, who trying to establish his credibility as someone who had recently been in practice as a teacher, once boasted about having pockets 'full of chalk dust' but unfortunately in an attempt to establish how hard he had worked as a teacher, linked this to an analogy between teachers and miners and boasted 'Unlike some colleagues I came into teacher education straight from the coal-face with my pockets still full of chalk dust'. Mixed metaphors are a sign that the writer has not thought too closely about what she is saying. Juxtaposing metaphors with contrasting images indicates that the words she is using do not arise from any image she has as she writes, that for her they are just convenient tools to make a resounding noise.

Cliché is as far as possible to be avoided in speech. More particularly, however, it is to be avoided when you write. Whereas when a person speaks, her direct contact with the audience allows them the opportunity to clarify whatever thought or emotion underpinned the use of a cliché, in writing this is not possible. So, for example, you should avoid the use of expressions such as 'at grass-roots level', 'at the sharp end' or 'at the coal-face'. The use of an expression such as 'in the cold light of day' to describe the way in which one is considering a problem or proposition is likely to add little to what one is trying to say. The use of the expression 'At this moment in time' (or worse, 'At this precise/particular/specific moment in time') to indicate that a problem is being addressed now as opposed to some other time is of course a redundancy since it is obvious that the individual is writing, or speaking, now and not at some other time. The use of expressions such as 'Give it your best shot' and 'Sock it to them' rather than 'Try to do your best'; 'You've got to get your act together' rather than 'You must try harder'; or 'I can't get my head round that' rather than 'I don't understand', is colourful but doesn't really add anything. Indeed, such colloquial clichés can become intensely irritating, which is why we do not feel bad about parodying the person who used to talk of coming from the coal-face with his pockets full of chalk dust.

We suggest that you make a list of clichés that you hear being used on radio or TV, or in the pub, or that you read in books or the papers. (Own up also to those clichés that you find yourself using in order to try to avoid their use.) When you have done this try putting as many of them as you can together in a short speech for an imaginary politician.

In Sections 2.14 and 2.15 we have discussed some of the dangers that lie in wait for unsuspecting students attempting to make sense in the English language. When they are at the same time anxious to impress their lecturers they are liable to fall into the various stylistic traps which we have discussed. If you wish to pursue this further you may care to read George Orwell's very instructive essay 'Politics and the English Language' (Orwell 1946) which discusses many aspects of poor writing in the English language better and in more detail than we do here.

# 2.16 Spelling

We cannot enter into a discussion of the rules of spelling; for that you will have to consult some other text. (See, for example, *Logical Spelling* by E. V. Allen, 1977.) However, it must be stressed that spelling is important in presenting yourself in writing.

Very often on reading drafts of students' work we will point out spelling errors and be assured that 'The final essay will have all that sorted out'. Unfortunately this is often untrue and essays arrive with many of the same errors as were present in the draft. Whether this is because the students in question simply cannot recognize a word that has been spelled wrongly when they see one or because they have failed to take the time to check their work thoroughly is unclear.

So we often find that students have problems with spelling and, what is more worrying, that they don't seem to see the importance of spelling accurately. One factor which may have contributed to both of these is the fashion that has been current in schools in recent years which has emphasized what is known as 'creative writing' at the expense of the craftsmanship of writing which includes spelling as well as grammar and punctuation. Someone who has been educated in this way may well think that our admonitions are either unnecessary or silly because spelling is less important than what they have to say. To them we would simply reiterate our warning that whatever attitude one's schoolteachers had to spelling, bad spelling creates a bad impression.

It is worthwhile getting a friend to read your essay with the intention of pointing out spelling errors and even places where she is unsure whether you have spelled a word correctly; you can check spellings she thinks are in doubt in a dictionary. Of course, you may not have a friend who is a decent speller but in general it is a good rule to ask someone else to check your work because she is less likely than you are to be so familiar with the text that she finds it difficult to concentrate on it at the level of spelling. When drafting and revising your work you should learn to read it in two ways. First you should be able to read it (as if you have never read it before) at the level of content. Does it make the points it is supposed to make? Does it make them succinctly and clearly? Secondly you should be able to read your work attending to format – to spelling, punctuation, grammar and so on.

Though the English language contains many irregular spellings there are some general rules that are worth learning. In this book we don't have space to go into such rules, many of which have important exceptions; such is the inconsistency in our use of the phonic system. For example, the rule most children learn to help them to spell words that contain the 'ee' sound made either with 'ei' or 'ie' – 'i before e except after c' – has important exceptions including, for example, 'caffeine', 'weird' and 'counterfeit'. For spelling rules you should consult a reliable text like that by

Allen to which we have already referred. What we want to do is simply to emphasize the importance of spelling if you want to make a good impression on your reader and then to draw your attention to some of the more common mistakes in spelling that we have come across.

If you know, or discover because you have a cruel (or kind) lecturer who points this out to you, that you frequently make spelling mistakes, you might care to write any words you frequently spell wrongly into a small notebook along with any spelling rules you learn. In this way you will at least learn which words you have most difficulty with and be able to check them whenever you use them.

Some of the most common spelling mistakes are to do with confusions between words that sound the same but are spelled differently and mean different things. A mistake with such a word can thus mean that you seem to be using one word when actually you intend to use another. The fact that words such as these sound the same can lead to confusions in spelling though a little thought should help you to avoid this. Words that sound the same but have different meanings are called homophones. Consider, for example:

principal, principle
there, their
practice, practise
compere, compare
two, too, to
know, no
threw, through
assent, ascent
pole, poll
tea, tee

Of this group of words 'practice' and 'practise' are particularly difficult since they refer to similar things, one being a noun and the other a verb. If you are keeping a notebook of spellings with which you have difficulty you may care to create a section on homophones and it would be a good exercise for you to write the meanings in alongside each of the above words; then add other homophones to them as you go along with the meanings written alongside.

Attending to how you speak is also important if you want to spell well. Slovenly speech can lead to gross errors in spelling. Here we are talking not only about the continued use of infantile versions of words such as 'kekkle' for 'kettle' and 'fing' for 'thing' but also to more complex oddities in language. Consider, for example, the boy from Oldham who, writing an account of the class trip to the zoo, wrote 'We all went ont buzz' (with 'buzz' being pronounced 'booz'). Here, apart from his transcription of the dialect contraction 'ont' for 'on the' he has spelled the word 'bus' like the word 'buzz' presumably because that is how he is used to saying the word 'bus'. Or consider the child who wrote 'Saw a great film at the weekend. Was naff good.' and continued 'You should of come with us.' Clearly in such a case the problem is not simply one about spelling but rather about the whole way in which language is being used to communicate. Though it may seem unlikely that adult students would make mistakes such as these, this just isn't true; recently one of us marked an essay in which a final year honours student made the mistake of using 'of' where 'have' was appropriate:

A teacher might not of been aware that he was indoctrinating . . .

For those who are fortunate enough to have access to a word processor, another thing to look out for is the possibility of spelling mistakes creeping in because you are writing too fast. For example, one of us frequently types 'peron' instead of 'person'. Mistakes such as these may remain in your final draft unless you develop the habit of reading your work carefully simply for spelling mistakes before deciding it is finished.

# 2.17  Success or failure?

When you have completed a piece of written work you must check that you have been successful. Always read through anything you have written before you decide that it is finished. Better still get someone else to read it for you. If she asks questions like 'What exactly is the point you're trying to make?', don't argue. Work out what you're trying to say and then try using new words to make the point; it's likely that in the earlier version you were being longwinded. One of us always asks his wife to read anything that he's written. Often she will say 'It's a bit long isn't it? What exactly is it that you're trying to say?' A moment's huffing and puffing with excuses like 'It's perfectly clear, what I'm saying is simply this . . .' followed by a short statement of intent after which comes the inevitable response: 'Then why don't you just say that? It would be so much clearer.' We suggest that whenever you've written something you get a friend to read it and try to tell you back what you've tried to say. If she can't understand what it is you are attempting to communicate, rewrite as much as is necessary to make your meaning clear to her. If there is no one you can ask, *imagine* the task of telling a friend the main points in your argument. This will help you to structure your writing and to decide upon content because it will allow you to pinpoint the key elements in your argument and to clarify the best order in which to present them. In structure, as in choice of words and phrases, it is better to be simple rather than complex, short rather than long.

# 2.18  Two common faults in essay writing

The single most common fault in essay writing is not addressing the question or topic properly; this is probably the most serious and common error in examinations also. You must read the question carefully and ensure that all aspects are addressed in your essay. You may decide to slant your essay towards one aspect or another of the question, in which case you should give good reasons for doing so. In the context of the examination hall another phenomenon sometimes comes into play. This is that of jumping the gun and beginning to write without sufficient thought as to whether what is being written is what is required, because you have stashed away in your mind a 'specimen' answer to a question, or a reasonably good memory of what you put into an earlier essay, and the exam question seems, on the surface, to be similar. Often the extent of similarity in such cases is not sufficient to warrant simply allowing the specimen answer or the old essay to pour onto the page unedited and we would advise strongly that you avoid this practice at all costs. Remember also that few examination questions or assignment tasks ask you to write down everything you know about a topic. They are usually much more specific and so you must learn to be selective in what you decide to write about.

Another common fault is that of regurgitating notes from lectures. This is unwise because it is unlikely that it is what is required. In addition, reading her own ideas is likely to be rather uninteresting for a lecturer and, as we have already suggested, though your job is partly to show that you can think and have some knowledge of your subject, it is also at least partly to interest your reader. A lecturer is likely to care about what she says and is unlikely to take well to what she has said being misrepresented. You should therefore be careful to be accurate in using ideas from lectures. In addition a lecturer would be justified in taking offence if you present her thoughts and ideas in an essay without acknowledging her ownership. This does not mean that you have to acknowledge every piece of information that you have gained from a lecturer; simply that when a lecturer has shared her own opinions, beliefs or arguments about some topic or about some other person's views, you should acknowledge that these ideas are hers if you use them.

# 2.19  What can you do to improve your writing?

In Part 2 we have tried to persuade you that it is worthwhile learning to write well as a student and we have looked at some ways in which you might approach writing which will increase your chances of doing so. Let us end by recapping briefly on some of the more important points we have made.

When you are writing as a student you should ensure that you address the topic without being side-tracked into issues that are only marginally relevant, however interesting. Your style and the words you use should be as simple as is compatible with making the points you wish to make. Remembering that the order in which you present ideas can make a great difference to whether you are successful in communicating, you should take care over the structure of what you write; taking care to use subheadings or other signposts to indicate the direction your essay is taking, will help.

You should be reflective about your work, reading critically what you have written, perhaps getting someone else to read drafts for you. In Part 1 we discussed different ways of reading and suggested the value of reading sympathetically. Reading others in this way is one very good way of improving your own writing – notice what works for other writers and try to allow that to influence your own style. Though we have emphasized the importance of sympathetic reading, you cannot assume that your readers will read your work sympathetically with a view to making sense. They may be keen to criticize it. So any writing you do as a student should be clear – avoid ambiguity and make sure that its structure helps rather than hinders the reader's understanding.

In Part 3 we will be looking at ways in which you might try to persuade others to accept a point of view you wish to defend; we will try to persuade you that rational means are in general to be preferred to non-rational ones.

# Part 3

## Developing Coherent Trains of Thought

In this part of the book we are going to show you how to construct your own arguments in your writing and also how to analyse and evaluate arguments that you come across in your reading. We will assume no prior knowledge of the nature of argument on your part but will rely on your common sense and willingness to take pains both in the construction of your own arguments and in the analysis of those used by others. We will pay particular attention to legitimate and illegitimate ways of persuading readers of a point of view. We are concerned to help you to put forward good reasons for the positions that you wish to adopt and to become adept at detecting whether or not good reasons are being adopted by authors whose work you read. We will alert you to the value of being fair as well as critical towards the material that you read. We will also discuss the differences that exist in constructing and criticizing arguments in speech on the one hand and in writing on the other.

You should learn to distinguish persuasion that takes place through the use of tricks or appeals to the emotions from persuasion that takes place through the offering of sound evidence and arguments for a belief. We recommend that you use the latter and become good at detecting and exposing the former.

Section 3.1 is concerned in a general way with the distinction between rational and non-rational forms of persuasion. We discuss different ways in which people try to persuade others to adopt a point of view using various doubtful strategies. Section 3.2 introduces you to the distinction between assertion and argument and gives you practice in recognizing different varieties and forms of argument. Section 3.3 gives you some practice in the evaluation of real arguments.

# 3.1 Influencing the beliefs of others

When we are setting out, developing or defending a position in our writing, we are hoping to induce in our readers a belief that what we are saying is true or at least plausible. In this section we will distinguish between ways of doing this that respect the rationality of those we are seeking to persuade and others that do not. One may give all the stylistic indications of setting out a case in a rigorous fashion, using devices such as: 'it follows from what I have just said', when in fact nothing follows; 'I have argued that . . .' when in fact no argument has been offered; 'I refute the suggestion that . . .' when the suggestion is merely contradicted, not argued against; 'it has been shown that . . .' when nothing of the kind has been done and so on, without actually setting out a case. Clearly the use of such phrases will often be justified when something has been demonstrated or does follow from what has been said or has been argued in favour of. However, the mere use of such expressions does not mean that what has been written is coherent or rigorous. A well-developed style is a good thing and can help to make a passage more persuasive, but it can also cover up for the fact that there is little substance beneath the stylistic glitter. Effective persuasion is not just a matter of style.

## Rational and non-rational forms of persuasion

Let us begin by distinguishing between rational and non-rational forms of persuasion. If I try to persuade you to believe something without attempting to give you any evidence for believing it or any good reason for believing it, then I have employed a non-rational form of persuasion. This will be the case even though there may be other, good reasons for believing it. Suppose, for example, that you very much want to become Vice-President of Ruritania, although you are endowed with only mediocre political abilities. If I persuade you to run for office because I tell you how brilliant you are and you accept my flattery, then you have been persuaded via appeals to your vanity rather than via your exercise of judgement. Given your ambition, there may still be independent rational reasons for running, at least from your point of view. For example, it may be that in Ruritania (and in some other countries) even a donkey would succeed in running for vice-president if he were to run for office with a popular presidential candidate; this would give you a rational basis for standing in the election. However, if you run because of my flattery, you run on non-rational grounds.

On the other hand, I may persuade you to believe something through what appears to be a rational argument even though it is not. (It is possible that I may not realize this myself.) For example, I may say that the Welsh Nationalists are going to win the general election because a recent poll of Gwynedd voters has shown them to be in the lead. (Why do I not have good grounds for my conclusion?) Perhaps my enthusiasm for the cause of Welsh Nationalism has led me to put forward this argument without pausing to consider the relative strength of Welsh Nationalism in Gwynedd compared to the rest of Britain. Again, you may assure me that I have chicken pox, because I have red spots on my face, on the grounds that anyone who has chicken pox, has red spots on their face. I may well have chicken pox, but this argument would not show it. Although my having red spots is *evidence* for my having chicken pox, it is not very strong evidence. On the other hand, having red spots is rather stronger evidence for my having some illness from a range of alternatives including chicken pox.

Sometimes showing someone evidence can persuade her in a rational way. This would be the case, for example, if a certain kind of scar is the only sign that a person has suffered a particular kind of snake-bite and he has such a scar. On the other hand, if the evidence we show him evokes an emotional response (where, for example, I use the photograph of a foetus aborted at the twenty-eighth week of pregnancy to persuade him that abortion is abhorrent), then it is arguably used as part of an attempt at non-rational persuasion. Where evidence is cast into a linguistic form it may serve as true premisses of an argument which may itself be good or bad. (By the term 'premiss' we mean the statements that in arguments are used to support conclusions. We will have more to say about them in Sections 3.2 and 3.3.) Thus the fact that John has red spots on his face serves as evidence for the truth of the statement 'John has red spots on his face', which may in turn, serve as a premiss in an argument. It is worth pointing out that in a written exposition it is rare that you will get a chance to show evidence directly. Instead, you will have to use statements about evidence as premisses in arguments that you are employing. It is therefore important that you do your best to put the reader in a position to *verify* the truth of those statements by providing the means of accessing the evidence (see Part 2 where we discuss citation). This shows once again the importance of citing sources of information, even when those sources may in themselves contain only indirect evidence.

It is not always possible to distinguish clearly between good and bad evidence. Nor is it always easy to distinguish between bad arguments and good arguments (the difference between good and bad arguments is discussed in Section 3.2). The important point is that you should make the attempt to provide good evidence or good arguments in favour of any position you wish to defend or advocate. At times, of course, despite the honest attempt to argue or give evidence in favour of your position, you will fail although you could not be accused of using non-rational means. For example, in the chicken pox case above, you would have attempted to present an argument to persuade me that I should see the doctor because of my chicken pox even though the argument you employed is a bad one.

So it is not always easy to distinguish between good and bad evidence or good and bad arguments. Nor is it always easy to distinguish between non-rational persuasion and rational persuasion. In Section 3.2 we deal with rational persuasion when we talk about the use of deductive and inductive arguments, and the legitimate use of arguments from authority. For the moment we want to consider some ways of persuading others that are illicit; most of these are examples of non-rational persuasion.


# Illicit ways of persuading others

There are many ways of persuading people to do something or to act in a certain way. Some of these are obviously unacceptable in a civilized society – the expression 'We have ways of making you talk' hints at the use of physical coercion in order to get a person to do something against her will. It is not so easy to get someone to change her beliefs as it is to get her to do something against her will. For example, by pointing a gun at a bank clerk I can make her open the safe. It would be much more difficult to get her to believe that it is right that I should appropriate the contents.

We will now examine a range of different ways in which the beliefs of others may be influenced by means that do not respect the rationality of the reader.


## *Indoctrination*

The term 'indoctrination' refers to a family of practices which are used to induce beliefs in others. We are particularly interested in written means of persuasion which fall within this family.

Indoctrination is a difficult process to describe in a thoroughly convincing way. A person who is indoctrinated is taught in such a way that her freedom to think independently about the material being taught is radically curtailed. This may arise either through the censorship of material prejudicial to the case the indoctrinator wishes to present, or by the selection only of material favourable to his own case. It is easy to see indoctrination taking place in an institutional setting such as a monastery,

military staff college or labour camp where influences that might under-
mine the indoctrination process can be rigorously excluded. It is important
to realize that it is still possible to indoctrinate (although perhaps in a less
thorough fashion) in a free and open setting through the one-sided
presentation of a case and through the exclusion of prejudicial material.
Consider this extract from a course booklet published in a college of higher
education. It is at least arguable that it is likely to be indoctrinatory:

> Black Women's Writing: We shall consider the nature of oppression in
> relation to gender and race.

This might be thought unexceptionable by many people because they
share the unstated assumption behind the prospectus, namely that all
women and black people are unjustly treated. However, because of their
general and undiscriminating nature, these assumptions ought to be
questioned rather than taken for granted. The *Oxford Paperback Dictionary*
(1988) definition of 'oppress' reads:

> to govern harshly, to treat with continual cruelty or injustice.

In the light of this definition the implications in the prospectus seem
more contentious. There is clearly a relationship between subordination
and oppression. If anyone is oppressed then she is in a subordinate position
in relation to her oppressor. However, it does not follow that if she is in a
subordinate position in relation to someone that she is oppressed by him.
What we have here is an example of question begging. The prospectus begs
the question of whether black women are oppressed; the fact that there is
no doubt that black people and women have occupied subordinate
positions throughout history does not necessarily mean that they have been
oppressed.

Many examples of indoctrinatory practices are to be found in an area
familiar to all of us, namely, advertising. Many advertisers at least attempt
to indoctrinate their audience. The fact that so many of them are doing so
at the same time tends, however, to cancel out the efforts of the others to a
certain extent. Moreover, advertisers are not always sure what it is about a
particular advertisement that proves effective. There is a story about an
advertising executive who, when told that only 50% of the money spent on
advertisements actually produced the right results, remarked that he
wished he knew which 50% that was.

## Failing to distinguish between fact and opinion

Presenting material in a way that could be considered as indoctrination is a
pitfall that teachers and writers, especially those strongly committed to
particular positions, need to beware of. In particular, they need to be very
careful about distinguishing between fact and opinion. Facts should be

presented as facts, opinions as opinions. Sometimes, knowledge of particular facts can be taken for granted if the writer can safely assume that the reader shares a degree of background knowledge. The author's own opinions should certainly not be taken for granted but should be made plain and distinguished carefully from the factual content of what is being stated. For example, although it can be safely assumed that nearly everyone in Britain over the age of 18 knows that Mrs Thatcher was once the Prime Minister, it *cannot* be assumed that everyone believes that she is incompetent. Generally speaking, it should be possible to distinguish between fact and opinion by asking yourself whether or not there is evidence to substantiate a factual claim. If there is not, then the information or point of view put forward should be indicated as the view of the author, rather than something for which there is clear evidence. For example, I may state:

> All the westbound number 11 buses were late yesterday at Lillie Road.

If I am able to give evidence of this by showing a log of actual times of arrival, compared with the advertised times of arrival, then even if I don't present the evidence in my text, I can put this statement forward as fact. I may wish to *cite* my evidence by giving a reference so that sceptical readers can check for themselves. Indeed I would be well advised to do so. Remember that in Section 1.1 we pointed out that in speech there is usually the opportunity for the listener to interject and ask for clarifications; this possibility does not exist for the writer. This means that if I assert that the number 11 bus is always late, and I do not have evidence for this assertion, I am not entitled to put forward my point of view as fact but only as my own opinion, hunch or guess.

## Terminological high jinks

In the last example we were dealing with the question as to whether or not a claim that is made is true. Such a question can be settled by *empirical investigation*, in other words, by observation and experiment. Not all disagreements can be settled in this way and a lot of opinions are not primarily about facts but about the meaning of certain words. In these cases, the question is not empirical but terminological. Before we can ask the question as to whether or not what the author states is true, we need to ask what she *means*.

Consider for example something that Tizard and Hughes say in a popular book on the language of 4-year-old children:

> Our transcripts suggest that young children are much less egocentric and illogical than Piaget believed.
>
> (Tizard and Hughes 1984, p. 126)

By 'egocentric' we would normally mean 'self-centred' or 'selfish'. However, Tizard and Hughes are using the word in a different sense to mean 'unable to see the world from the viewpoint of another person'. One of the examples the authors use to back up their contention that children are less egocentric than Piaget believed, is of a child asking how Father Christmas knows which address particular children live at. In this case, the child is seeing a possible problem from the point of view of Father Christmas. Using this as an example of a child not being egocentric might seem odd to someone who is unaware of the special meaning Tizard and Hughes are attaching to the word 'egocentric' because it is an example of a child being able to see another person's point of view rather than being unselfish. However, if the way in which 'egocentric' is being used in the context of this discussion of child development was explained, what at first sight appeared to be an odd example would be shown to be perfectly comprehensible. What we have here is a *terminological* confusion or a confusion as to the meanings of words used.

The last example showed the importance of not making the assumption that your readers will be familiar with technical uses of otherwise familiar vocabulary. We discuss this at some length in the section on jargon in Part 2. It is even more important to avoid confusing fact and opinion. To return to the example of 'the nature of oppression in relation to gender and race' on p. 106, it can be argued that the fact/opinion distinction is not being carefully observed there. It would, no doubt, have been justifiable to talk about the subordination of women but this would not have carried the same impact as talking of 'oppression'. Oppression and subordination as we have already noted are related to one another. But 'subordination' does not carry with it the pejorative overtones of 'oppression' and for that reason does not have the same impact because it does not contain within itself the connection with *injustice* that the definition of 'oppression' clearly does. The need for an *argument* for the view that the relationship between some races and between the sexes embodies injustice is thus apparently made redundant by begging the question of whether black women are oppressed. It is only by noticing and insisting on the difference between terms like 'oppression' and 'subordination' that one is able to expose such a move. People who use terminology in the way 'oppression' has been used in the above example, will complain that we are nit-picking by making such distinctions; they will do this because by their terminological high jinks they seek to persuade others of their own favoured point of view. You should not be deflected by this kind of criticism, however, if you are satisfied that an important distinction that should be made has not been made.

## Sophistry

Sophistry is a group of techniques named after the Classical Greek teachers known as the Sophists who made their living by instructing citizens in the art of persuasion. In the small city-states such as Athens that existed in Classical Greece, all free, adult, male citizens had the right to take part in government. Since the number of citizens would only be several thousand at the most, it was possible to run the city-states through direct participation without the need to elect a parliament. Needless to say, an active citizen who wanted to be influential in the affairs of his state would be influential to the extent that he was able to persuade large numbers of his fellow citizens to his point of view. The Sophists had clearly identified what might nowadays be called a 'market niche' for the particular skills they were selling: those citizens who wished to gain friends and influence people in the public assemblies and law courts of their city-states. In such a situation neither brainwashing nor indoctrination could readily have been used. Something different was called for.

Part of what the Sophists taught is what is known as 'oratory' or the art of speaking effectively in public. This is an art still practised by politicians, although it has become tailored very much to the requirements of television rather than the political platform. The other aspect of their programme is more directly relevant to our concerns. Many of the Sophists attempted to teach their pupils techniques of argument which could be applied irrespective of the subject matter being discussed. These techniques were tailored to the end of persuading an audience and were to be judged by their effectiveness in doing that. As far as most of the Sophists were concerned, the ends justified the means, irrespective of whether or not they employed good evidence or sound arguments. If your technique for persuading people to believe something worked then it was a good technique. If it did not work, then it was not a good technique. This part of the package is known today as *sophistry* when it employs bad forms of reasoning. Here is an example of the techniques the Sophists often used, recorded by Plato. The scene is a dialogue between the philosopher Socrates and some of his companions. They are meeting Dionosydorus, a Sophist, who is giving a demonstration of his technique. Socrates records the encounter:

Dionosydorus: Tell me, Socrates and the rest of you who say that you want this young man to become wise, are you in jest or in real earnest?

Socrates:
(aside) I was led by this to imagine that they fancied us to have been jesting when we asked them to converse with the youth themselves, and that this made them jest and play, and being under this impression I was the more decided in saying that we were in profound earnest.

Dionosydorus: Reflect, Socrates: you may have to deny your words.

Socrates: I have reflected and I shall never deny my words.

Dionosydorus: Well, and so you say you wish Cleinias to become wise?

Socrates: Undoubtedly.

Dionosydorus: And is he already wise or not?

Socrates: At least his modesty would not allow him to say that he is.

Dionosydorus: You wish him to become wise and not to be ignorant?
Socrates:     That we do.
Dionosydorus: You wish him to become what he is not, and no longer
              be what he is?

*Socrates is thrown into consternation at this move of Dionosydorus, who takes
advantage and adds*

Dionosydorus: You wish him no longer to be what he is, which can
              only mean that you wish him to perish. Pretty lovers
              and friends they must be who want above all other
              things that their favourite should perish!
              (Based on *The Dialogues of Plato*: Euthydemus, p. 149)

It is easy enough to see that a dubious move has been made by
Dionosydorus, less easy to state precisely what it is. What Dionosydorus
seems to be doing is making out that *any* property of a person is essential to
his or her existence, so that any change that occurs in Cleinias will result in
his being Cleinias no longer, which is clearly absurd. Detecting the
absurdity and explaining it clearly in the context of an argument is,
however, a matter that requires considerable skill and confidence. It was an
ability to confuse and disorient their pupils and opponents through the use
of tricks like this that gave the Sophists such an influence.

## Persuading by non-rational means

We want now to discuss some dubious techniques that people often use in
attempting to convince others of the rightness of their opinions. These are
all techniques that we would argue against using. Convincing others by
using them does not show how right you are, it simply shows how cleverly
you can box with words. It is likely that after reading about these you will
realize that you have been using the same or similar techniques in your
writing to date. This does not necessarily mean that you have been using
them deliberately because it is quite possible to use them and be unaware of
doing so. We suggest that you pay close attention to your writing and try as
far as possible to avoid these techniques. We have adopted the expression
'persuader' to refer to words and phrases that illicitly persuade someone to
accept a point of view, 'crafty conflation' to refer to a particular way of
confusing the meanings of words, and the notion of the 'You won't believe
this' challenge, from Oswald Hanfling's excellent block on the uses and
abuses of argument in the Open University course A101 (Hanfling 1978).
    Here are some of the main techniques to look out for:

(i)    Assertions posing as arguments.
(ii)   The use of emotive language.
(iii)  The use of 'persuader' words and phrases.
(iv)   The crafty conflation.

(v)   Begging the question.
(vi)   The 'You won't believe this' challenge.
(vii)   Rash generalization.

## (i) Assertions posing as arguments

Sometimes writers make a series of assertions which they surround with verbal devices that suggest they are supported by arguments. For example, they might write, 'I will argue that . . .' or 'I will employ an argument for the belief that . . .' or claim to have used arguments when in fact no argument is offered. In Part 2 we warned against claiming to offer an argument when you do not. Remember that there is a difference between arguing for a point of view and asserting it; you should be clear about when you are simply stating an opinion or belief and when you are arguing in its support or offering evidence in its favour.

## (ii) Emotive language

Sometimes writers use emotive language to try to persuade a reader into accepting a point of view that she otherwise might reject. Emotive language may well refer to the same individuals, events, things or properties of things, as more neutral language. However, it differs by exciting a reaction of approval or animosity in the listener or reader through the associations that it evokes. The use of expressions such as 'rabble' for 'crowd' or 'riot' for 'demonstration' would be examples of the use of this technique, as would the use of 'workshy layabout' for 'unemployed person' and 'baby' for 'embryo' or 'foetus'. Those who referred to peaceful citizens exercising their civil right to demonstrate in the Poll Tax demonstration in London in April 1990 as 'rioters' and 'Marxist rabble-rousers' sought, by doing so, to turn the public eye away from the serious nature of resistance to the Community Charge.

It is not always obvious which uses of language are emotive. For example, those who are pro-choice in the matter of abortion would argue that to refer to foetuses as 'babies' is to try illicitly to persuade through the use of emotive language. But while no doubt it could legitimately be claimed that some anti-abortionists who use such language intend no more than to fire emotion about 'the inhuman and evil slaughter of innocent babies', some at least use the word 'babies' in a non-emotive way to refer to those who, through careful thought, they have concluded are best referred to in this way. By contrast, some anti-abortionists would argue that the claim that any interference in women's 'right to choose' would result in the 'criminalization' of many women who seek nothing more than to have power over their own lives, is to use emotive language illicitly to persuade people to legalize the killing of unborn babies.

*Exercise*
Look out for uses of emotive language: in the newspapers, in the electronic media, in the pub. Particularly rich sources of examples are likely to arise whenever people are campaigning for something in which they believe very strongly.

## (iii) The use of persuaders

By persuader words and phrases, we mean words and phrases that are put into an assertion illicitly to persuade the reader to accept what is said, by other than rational means. A writer may or may not be conscious that she is using 'persuaders'. Perhaps the best way to illustrate this technique is to give you some examples of persuaders and for you to pick them out of the sentences below.

(a)  Surely all teachers must realize that their job is one of the most important in the country.
(b)  We have to remember that the Soviet Union is just waiting for an opportunity to expand into Western Europe and so we have to maintain our first strike nuclear capability.
(c)  Only a fool could fail to see that Mrs Thatcher was the best Prime Minister the country has ever had.
(d)  It is perfectly obvious to anyone with a modicum of sense that this country has never had such an incompetent, inhumane or disastrous Prime Minister as Mrs Thatcher.
(e)  It has to be admitted that whatever the risks that nuclear weapons bring, without them we would not have had peace for over forty years.
(f)  We cannot go on using up the earth's resources at this rate and expect mankind to survive as a civilized species beyond the twenty-first century; this much is manifestly clear.

*Exercise*
What persuaders are used in these examples?

'Surely'; 'We have to remember'; 'Only a fool could fail to see'; 'It is perfectly obvious that'; 'It has to be admitted that'; 'This much is manifestly clear'.

Persuaders are used to suggest that the point being made is obvious, that it needs no argument. They are used to persuade listeners and readers to accept as undeniable statements which are perhaps quite doubtful.

*Exercise*
Write a list of persuader words and phrases with some examples of their use.

*Here is our list*

Surely, plainly, obviously, clearly, self-evidently, undeniably, manifestly, naturally, it has to be admitted that, it is manifestly obvious, everyone must, we have to remember, I need hardly remind you, as you will agree, it is true that, it is a fact that, everyone will have had the experience that, no one would deny the fact that, only a fool would fail to realize.

When someone uses such words or phrases as persuaders she is trying to trick others into accepting unsupported assertions. By asserting that 'plainly' or 'obviously' or 'clearly' or 'undeniably' something is the case, she is trying to make the listener or reader agree. If it is *plainly* or *obviously* or *clearly* or *undeniably* so, then the listener or reader would have to be rather foolish not to see it; and who wants to admit to himself that he is foolish?

It is important to notice that the context in which a word or phrase that could serve as a persuader is used is important in determining whether or not it is being used as a persuader. For example, we could say 'All students at Cartrefle are expected to attend lectures. This is undeniably true.' Are we using a persuader here? Not all uses of words or phrases that might in certain contexts be seen as persuaders are necessarily devious.

Such phrases can be used in an acceptable manner if they are properly supported by argument or evidence. For example the statement: 'Members of the caring professions face moral decisions every day. This is undeniably true', could be used in connection with firm evidence that members of professions such as social work and nursing do face moral decisions daily. In this case the phrase 'this is undeniably true' would not be serving as a persuader but rather as a mark of emphasis.

Let us make one last point about a very commonly used kind of persuader. These are cases where appeals are made to science. It is worthwhile looking for statements such as: 'Modern science has shown . . .' or 'According to physics . . .'. Such appeals are often accompanied by references to famous scientific personalities. The idea is that science, which is supposed to be objective (and hence fair, honest and reliable), is the best arbiter of any claim to human knowledge. But apart from the fact that this isn't true as anyone who has studied science at a reasonable level will know (did you spot the persuader in that comment?), appeals to science, unless they are backed up by a detailed account of the way in which the conclusion was reached, are no more reliable than any other kind of appeal. This is an example of an appeal to authority and in this case it is not a justified one. You should note, however, that some appeals to authority are unavoidable and justified; we will look at such cases in Section 3.2.

## (iv) Crafty conflation

This is one of the most commonly employed tricks. Crafty conflation involves running together or conflating a number of ideas which in spite of their similarities and connections, are actually distinct, often meaning very different things.

For instance, in writing an essay a student may wish to assert that something (call it A) is the case but have some doubt about whether he can simply assert it. If he can't really find a way of arguing for it he may resort to craftily conflating because he knows that it would be safe to assert B. In the end he may write: 'A, in other words B', thus implying that A and B are the same thing.

When someone uses crafty conflation, she slides from one word or phrase to another, as if the two phrases were one and the same. In general, crafty conflation can take these forms:

A, in other words B.

A, that is to say, B.

A or B.

or even simply

A, B.

Here are some examples of crafty conflation:

Securing equal opportunities for ethnic minorities, in other words, an anti-racist policy.

The best Prime Minister this country has every had, that is to say, Mrs Thatcher.

Children should learn to read using stimulating reading material or real books.

Ladies and gentlemen, the greatest rock and roll band in the world, the Rolling Stones.

Totalitarian communist regimes are collapsing like ninepins all over Eastern Europe. Socialism can no longer claim any validity as a form of political organization.

*Exercise*
Try making up your own examples of crafty conflation. And try to spot occasions when people you are speaking to, or authors you read, use this method of illicit persuasion.

## (v) Begging the question

By 'begging the question' we mean one of two things. Strictly speaking to 'beg the question' is to offer an argument in which the conclusion to be argued for is already stated in the premises. The phrase is also used more generally to apply to cases where something questionable is taken for granted. Crafty conflations are one way of begging the question because they take it for granted that two assertions mean much the same, even though this is questionable.

One indication that someone might be begging the question comes when he uses words and phrases like 'remember', 'point out', 'see' and 'remind'. If we remind someone of something, point it out to her, or ask her whether she remembers it, we take it for granted that what we remind her about, point out to her, or enquire whether she remembers, really is as we say it is. For example:

(a)   Someone might say 'You'll remember that water is lighter than air'. There is a presupposition here not only that water is lighter than air but that you know that it is (of course this presupposition is actually false!). You can't legitimately be asked whether you remember that something is the case unless it actually is the case.

(b)   Someone might say 'I pointed out to him that there were more road deaths in 1985 than there had been in 1983'. She might be justified in pointing this out because, as a matter of fact, there were more road deaths in 1985 than there had been in 1983. However, it would be possible for her to talk of 'pointing it out' even though this was untrue. To use the form of words that she has used presupposes that there really were more deaths in 1985 than in 1983.

(c)   Here is an example that teachers often use: 'Why did you talk just now, Smith?' This presupposes that Smith actually did talk just now. This is like the classic 'Are you still beating your wife?'

(d)   If someone asks you whether or not you saw a man with a bag marked 'swag' running from the bank, this presupposes that there really was a man with a bag marked 'swag' running from the bank for you to see. Something similar is true with the word 'know'. For example, a friend could ask 'Did you know that President Bush was attending the same mental hospital for outpatient treatment as Mrs Thatcher?'

(e)   A committed vegetarian might ask you, as you are eating your T-bone steak, 'You are aware, aren't you, that people who eat meat are five times more likely to die of heart disease than vegetarians?'

It is important, when you are writing, to avoid begging the question. It is equally important, when you are reading, or listening to others speaking, to notice when they are begging the question.

*Exercise*
Try to spot examples of question begging that you come across in your reading, on radio and television, and in the conversations you have. Speeches by politicians (when they make sense) are a particularly rich source of examples of question begging.

## (vi) The 'You won't believe this' challenge

The 'You won't believe this' challenge relies upon the tendency of people to believe an incredible story more readily than one that is merely unlikely

(Hanfling 1978). The challenge may be put in several ways: 'You are never going to believe this . . .'; 'Of course most people find it hard to accept that . . .'; 'I know that your intuition will be to reject what I have to say . . .'.

When someone uses such phrases she is often asking you either to accept her assertions or to admit to being a narrow-minded person who cannot face facts, or who cannot rise above intuition to see the truth of what he is saying. Such a person, it is implied, so lacks imagination that he is not prepared to believe new ideas just because they are well, unbelievable.

The fact that someone uses a form of words that approximates to the 'You won't believe this' challenge does not necessarily mean that we should reject what she says. Many facts now taken for granted have seemed unbelievable to people in the past. Just be alert when this form of words is used.

*Exercise*
Try out the YWBT challenge on a few of your friends. How outrageous a point of view or alleged fact can you get them to accept? Try to avoid the challenge in your written work.

## (vii) Rash generalization and universal statements

Sometimes writers use rather bold statements that are quite unwarranted such as 'Everyone knows that . . .', 'It is commonly believed that . . .', or 'Many people would argue that . . .'. The use of generalizations of this kind can be rather rash and when used by a student may result in marks in the margin of an essay such as these: 'Actually, I don't know this; in fact, I don't even believe it!', 'I don't know anyone who believes this', or 'Who would argue it?'

Rash generalizations are often quite unsupported by facts although they appear to be claims of a factual kind. It is better to make a less bold statement or at least to give some evidence for the generalizations that you use. For example, if you do want to claim that many people would argue something, you should give references to some who do.

Not all generalizations are rash. A generalization can be supported by good evidence or it can be a restatement of what is already claimed by a number of statements about individuals. For example, if I know that it is true of each parliamentary seat in Scotland that the Tories do not hold it, I can assert, 'There are no Tory MPs in Scotland'.

# 3.2 Arguments of different kinds

We are all familiar with arguments in the sense of people airing their differences of opinion. They are most likely to do so through face-to-face disagreement. Arguments in this sense can range from a civilized exchange of views through heated discussion to bad-tempered shouting that stops just short of fighting. Typically, an argument in this common sense of the word involves the conflict of opposing points of view. Participants will attempt to persuade others of their own point of view by *asserting* what they wish others to believe, and by presenting *evidence* and *reasons* in its favour. When reasons are presented for a point of view, we have the basis for an argument in its favour. We will restrict our use of the term 'argument' to refer to the giving of reasons for points of view. When we wish to refer to arguments in the more common sense of the word, we will use the expression 'disagreement'.

In Section 3.2 we will begin by discussing the difference between argument and assertion. Then we will say a little about the nature of argument in general and about deductive and inductive arguments in particular. Finally, we will discuss arguments from authority which may be seen as a particular species of inductive argument.

## Argument and assertion

There is a distinction between arguing for a point of view and merely asserting it. Imagine that you believe that something is true and further that you want to persuade someone else to believe that it is true. Say, for example, that you believe Bruce Springsteen is a brilliant guitarist and that you wish to persuade someone of this. How might you go about it?

Asserting that Springsteen is a brilliant guitarist would involve merely stating something of this kind:

Bruce Springsteen is a brilliant guitarist!

This assertion may persuade some people to believe that Springsteen is a brilliant guitarist but notice that in making it you have not offered any reasons why they should. If, in addition to making the assertion you were to offer reasons then you would be offering an argument. For example, you might say:

Bruce Springsteen is a brilliant guitarist because he plays very fast and my friend who plays in a band says so and he's a great guitarist.

This is an argument in favour of the assertion that Springsteen is a brilliant guitarist. Notice, however, that its being an argument does not mean that it is a good argument. (What would make it a good argument?)

Later in this part we will be discussing the question of what makes the difference between good and bad arguments. For the moment it is important to distinguish clearly between argument and assertion. In arguing a case we offer reasons and sometimes evidence for the point we are making. In asserting something, on the other hand, we offer no reasons, we simply say that such and such is the case.

It is usually not enough simply to assert something to be the case. Of course, in arguing a case, we will invite others to accept some assertions that we make and on the basis of these we will build up our argument. So we're not saying that you should never make assertions, only that assertion on its own is rarely good enough. In general, offering arguments is superior to simply making assertions.

If you assert something to be the case I might say; 'Well, very interesting, but why should I believe that?' Unless what you assert is so reasonable that anyone who knows what you are talking about would accept it (and of course many assertions are of this kind), if you don't go on to give me reasons (that is, to offer to justify your assertion by giving an argument in its favour), I may very well reject it. Arguments have a structure which allows us to see how the statement to be upheld or asserted is backed up by reasons. The statement to be upheld or asserted is called the *conclusion* and the statements on which it is based are known as *premisses*. In offering an argument you are giving me reasons for believing something, provided that the premisses are true.

There is a very well-known argument which goes:

All men are mortal.
Socrates is a man.
Therefore: Socrates is mortal.

In this argument the first two lines are the premisses and the part of the third line that comes after 'Therefore' and follows from the premisses, is known as the conclusion.

*Exercise*
What are the premisses and conclusions in these arguments?

All Manchester policemen are racists.
David White is a Manchester policeman.
Therefore certainly: David White is a racist.

Nearly all Scottish philosophers are handsome.
G.F. is a Scottish philosopher.
Therefore probably: G.F. is handsome.

In the first example (which is a deductive argument) the conclusion of the argument is that David White is a racist; in the second (which is an example of inductive argument) the conclusion is that G.F. is handsome. In each example the other statements are the premisses.

Notice that in the above arguments we have used 'Therefore certainly . . .' and 'Therefore probably . . .' to indicate respectively a deductive and an inductive argument the nature of which we will discuss below. Normally these would be replaced simply by 'therefore' and it would be for the reader to decide whether in the given context the argument was deductive or inductive. In the deductive case 'therefore' would always stand for 'therefore certainly'. In the inductive case on the other hand, 'therefore' would stand for a continuum ranging between 'Therefore it is almost certain that . . .' through 'Therefore there is a very good chance that . . .' to 'Therefore there is some possibility that . . .'. Which of these was true would depend on the strength of the first premiss which might claim, for example, that '99.9% of' or 'a very large number of' or 'some' Scottish philosophers are handsome.

Although it is possible to set out arguments so that the relationship between premisses and conclusions is made clear, when arguments develop in the course of a disagreement, this relationship is often much less clear. There are a number of reasons for this which are worth looking at before we consider the setting out of arguments on the printed page.

In a disagreement, the point a person is attempting to defend is usually set forth first and, as it is challenged, reasons are given to back it up. At the same time the other party or parties are trying to defend their own point of view, which is usually opposed to that of the first party. So, very often, there are at least two arguments developing within a disagreement. Disagreements usually develop on an unplanned basis, and so therefore the arguments which they express develop in a haphazard way. Finally, an argument developed in the course of a disagreement very often contains gaps, both in the intermediate steps, and in the premisses on which it rests. These are discussed below. This is because when one is involved in a disagreement one very often assumes that the person with whom one is arguing understands the premisses on which one's argument is based, so that there is no need to make them explicit.

Let us now say a little about the distinction between deductive and inductive arguments and their characteristics.

# Deductive arguments

It is the main characteristic of deductive arguments that they are used to establish their conclusions as certainly true *given the truth of the premisses.* *Deductive arguments* are either *valid* or *invalid.* In a valid argument the conclusion follows from the premisses. A valid deductive argument cannot have a false conclusion if its premisses are all true. Given a true premiss or premisses and a valid argument you can *prove* the conclusion. Validity is an 'all or nothing' affair. There are no degrees of validity and a deductive argument is either valid or invalid.

Consider again the argument about David White:

All Manchester policemen are racists.
David White is a Manchester policeman.
Therefore: David White is a racist.

This is a valid argument. If all Manchester policemen are racists and if David White is a Manchester policeman then he must be a racist. Notice, however, that one or other of the premisses could be false without affecting the validity of the argument.

In an invalid argument the conclusion does not follow from the premisses. Invalid arguments can lead from true premisses to false conclusions. Let us suppose that it is true that if you have chicken pox you are covered in red spots and let us further suppose that Darren is covered in red spots. Someone may be tempted to argue:

If you have chicken pox you are covered in red spots.
Darren is covered in red spots.
Therefore: Darren has chicken pox.

This argument is invalid. Even if the premisses are true the conclusion may be false because the form of the argument is invalid; valid and invalid forms of argument are discussed below. Darren may have red spots but be suffering from measles. Even the fact that Darren had chicken pox would not mean that this argument was valid, because its conclusion does not follow from its premisses.

*Exercise*
Here are two more examples of invalid arguments. Why do you think that they are invalid?

All whales are mammals.
Some mammals are sea-going.
Therefore: All whales are sea-going.

All shopkeepers eat sweets.
Some sweets are harmful to the teeth.
Therefore: All shopkeepers eat sweets that are harmful to the teeth.

The first of these arguments leads from two true premisses to a true conclusion but the conclusion does not follow from the premisses. The second goes from one false premiss (not all shopkeepers eat sweets!) and one true premiss, to a false conclusion and again the conclusion does not follow from the premisses.

In order to see that the first argument is invalid, try substituting 'voles' for 'whales'. You will then have an argument of the same form which leads from true premisses to a false conclusion. You will also be able to see much more clearly that the conclusion does not follow from the premisses.

In order to see that the second argument is invalid, try substituting 'orchestral players play' for 'shopkeepers eat', 'musical instruments' for 'sweets' and 'trumpets' for 'harmful to the teeth'. You will then have an argument which is the same in form as the shopkeepers example, but which leads from true premisses to false conclusions.

So far we have been discussing relatively short and simple arguments. Sometimes, however, arguments are more complex. At times an argument is made up of several smaller arguments the conclusions of which then serve as premisses in the next step in the larger argument; these are known as 'intermediate steps' in the larger argument. Very often they are not stated in the course of a disagreement or a discussion because it is assumed, rightly or wrongly, that the other person grasps the moves implicitly. In a disagreement it is possible for a listener to interrupt and ask for amplification of a particular argument and thus have intermediate steps spelled out. You should notice that intermediate steps are often left out of written arguments also. The difference in a written argument is, of course, that there is no direct opportunity to ask for amplification. Let us consider the development of an argument as it might grow in the course of a conversation, in order to show how intermediate steps may be spelled out as the discussion proceeds.

We may argue:

John is a Falkland Islander.
Therefore: John does not need a visa to visit Britain.

Here we have connected a premiss to a conclusion and produced the basis of an argument. This may be enough for someone well acquainted with the status of the Falkland Islands. However, someone who is not, may ask for further elucidation. She will not be able to see how this conclusion follows from this simple premiss. We may now add the further premiss:

All Falkland Islanders are British Citizens.

For most people this would be enough to allow them to see how the conclusion follows from the premisses. However, it may still not be enough for our listener so we may add by way of further elucidation:

No British Citizen needs a visa to visit Britain.

Is the argument satisfactory now with the two additional premisses? Most people would say 'yes', but it would still be possible to point out that the argument is not complete, not through lack of premisses, but because, given these three premisses, the conclusion still does not follow from them. Another intermediate step needs to be filled in first. This step is: From the premiss that John is a Falkland Islander and the premiss that All Falkland

Islanders are British Citizens, it follows that John is a British citizen. This step allows us to conclude that John does not need a visa to visit Britain.

The complete argument now looks like this:

John is a Falkland Islander. (premiss)
All Falkland Islanders are British citizens. (premiss)
So, John is a British citizen. (intermediate step)
No British citizen needs a visa to visit Britain. (premiss)
Therefore, John does not need a visa to visit Britain. (conclusion)

The intermediate step in this argument follows from the first two premisses and so can best be seen as a conclusion of a smaller argument within the main argument. Many arguments consist of substages of this kind. Remember that arguments of this kind are *deductive* arguments. That is, if the premisses are true, then the conclusion must be true if it is a valid argument.

Remember that the validity of an argument has nothing to do with whether its premisses are true. Both valid and invalid arguments can lead from true premisses to true conclusions, from false premisses to true conclusions, and from false premisses to false conclusions. However, valid arguments, unlike invalid arguments, never lead from true premisses to false conclusions. A valid argument with true premisses is said to prove its conclusion.

Deductive arguments are said to be valid or invalid in virtue of their form, rather than the truth or falsity of their premisses. Whether or not a particular argument is valid or invalid depends on whether or not its form is valid or invalid. The idea of the form of an argument will become clearer with some more examples.

*Exercise*
Consider the following argument:

All men are beasts.
Darren is a man.
Therefore: Darren is a beast.

(a) Write down what you take to be the premiss or premisses of the argument.
(b) Write down what you take to be the conclusion of the argument.
(c) Is the argument valid?
(d) Are the premisses true?
(e) Does the argument prove the conclusion?

*Discussion*
(a) The premisses are 'All men are beasts' and 'Darren is a man'.
(b) The conclusion is 'Darren is a beast'.
(c) The argument is valid.

(d) The first premiss is plainly false since we know at least two men who are not beasts; we cannot speak for Darren's beastliness or non-beastliness.
(e) No, because at least one of the premisses is false. Remember that this would be the case even if Darren *was* a beast.

*Exercise*
Consider the following argument:

> If you are a Scottish millionaire then you have lots of money.
> You have lots of money.
> Therefore: You are a Scottish millionaire.

(a) Write down what you take to be the premiss or premisses of the argument.
(b) Write down what you take to be the conclusion of the argument.
(c) Suppose that the premisses and the conclusion are true, is the conclusion thereby proved?

*Discussion*
(a) The premisses are 'If you are a Scottish millionaire then you have lots of money' and 'You have lots of money'.
(b) The conclusion is 'You are a Scottish millionaire'.
(c) The conclusion is not proved since the argument is invalid even though both the premisses and the conclusion may be true.

You may wish to return to this example after finishing the chapter and try constructing an argument of the same form which leads from true premisses to a false conclusion.

## Seeing similarities among arguments

Recognizing that arguments have the same form requires practice. There are a number of very common valid and invalid forms which it is possible to learn to recognize; doing so would help you to understand better what is involved in setting out arguments. Those who wish to go deeper into examples of valid and invalid forms should look at Salmon (1963), Chapter 2.

Look again at the argument about Darren. Is the following argument of the same form?

> All Northamptonians are friendly.
> Rosina is a Northamptonian.
> Therefore: Rosina is friendly.

This argument shares the same *form* as that about Darren and both are valid in virtue of that form. We can see that they have this common form by removing what is particular to them and leaving what is common. Thus, in the first premiss of the Darren argument we will remove 'men' and 'beasts';

in the second premiss we will remove 'Darren' and 'man' and in the conclusion we will remove 'Darren' and 'beast'. Replacing these words with the letters, A, B and C we get:

All As are B.
C is an A.
Therefore: C is a B.

*Exercise*
Try substituting A, B and C for what is particular in the Rosina example in order to satisfy yourself that it has the same valid form as the Darren example.

# Inductive arguments

It is important to realize that by no means all arguments are deductive. Just as important as deductive arguments, are *inductive* arguments. Unlike deductive arguments, they do not have the properties of validity and invalidity, although they may be *sound* or *unsound*. Sound arguments give you good reasons for believing the conclusion given that the premisses are true and unsound arguments do not. Consider the following example:

Nearly all travellers will reach their destination safely.
Roberta is a traveller.
Therefore probably: Roberta will reach her destination safely.

This is an example of a sound inductive argument. The premisses give us good grounds for accepting the conclusion. We have good grounds for *believing* the conclusion if the premisses are true. With induction the argument may be sound, the premisses true and the conclusion false. What we can say is that the premisses support, to a degree, the conclusion.

As we have seen, sometimes the conclusion of an inductive argument is prefaced with 'probably'. This indicates that we are advancing the conclusion with a certain degree of caution. The term 'probably' is not part · of the argument, but is an indication that the argument being used is an inductive rather than a deductive one.

In the case of induction the premisses will support the conclusion to varying degrees. For example, if the first premiss of the above argument was changed to:

Most travellers reach their destination safely.

we would be inclined to say that the conclusion is now supported a little less strongly than in the first case, although it is still supported. This is because 'most' means any quantity greater than half of the total whereas 'nearly all' suggests a much larger proportion. The *content* of an inductive argument is, therefore, important. The nature of the premisses affects the soundness of the argument. Sometimes the premisses in an inductive argument have a numerical value. For example, if the premiss:

99.9% of travellers reach their destination safely.

was substituted for the first premiss, it would make the argument more sound than substituting:

80% of travellers reach their destination safely.

Those readers who have studied or are studying the social sciences will already have realized that many arguments in subjects like sociology or politics are inductive in nature. Unlike deduction, where it is the form of the argument that determines its validity, in induction, the number and content of the premisses influences the degree of soundness or un-soundness we are prepared to allow it. For example, most people would not be prepared to accept the following as a sound inductive argument:

0.01% of the electorate were asked how they would vote if there were a general election held tomorrow. .
90% of those asked said they would vote Conservative.
Therefore: The Conservatives would win an election if it were held tomorrow.

Can you work out why most social scientists would reject this argument as unsound?

*Discussion*
The reason is that no indication is given as to whether the sample of voters who were asked is in any sense representative. If on the other hand the argument gave details about how the sampling had been carried out most social scientists might form a different opinion of it. If, for example, the following additional premiss was added:

Those asked constituted a random stratified sample of the electorate.

those of us who understand that random stratified sampling is a statistical method of achieving the best possible prediction, would happily accept the argument as more sound than it was before even if the rest of the argument remained unchanged (see Smith 1981, Chapter 6). If on the other hand the additional premiss was:

The names of those asked were drawn from a register of Conservative Party members.

most people with a modicum of sense would realize that the argument was less sound as a result of adding this premiss.

In sampling theory, the way in which the sample is selected and the size of the sample are as important as the proportion of the population that the sample represents in influencing our willingness to accept the soundness of an argument. The example further illustrates that the addition of extra premisses to an inductive argument may increase or decrease the level of its soundness. This again contrasts induction with deduction, where the addition of premises will not affect the form of the argument, assuming of course that when we come to evaluate it, any hidden premises have been made overt.

# Arguments from authority

None of us is an expert in every subject. Even in those subjects where we can lay claim to some knowledge, we are not infallible. However, because of this very situation we are obliged, if we wish to gain reliable information about subjects about which we know little or nothing, to consult *experts* or *authorities*. If someone states that such and such is the case; for example, if they were to assert that 'It will rain in Perth tomorrow', we would not normally accept that it will rain merely on that person's say so unless she is a recognized authority on the area in question, in this case, the weather. The reason for this lies in the distinction between *argument* and *assertion*, which was discussed at the beginning of Part 3. To use symbolism similar to that used earlier when showing the form of certain particular deductive arguments: if Peter says that p (where p is any statement), we do not accept p without evidence or further argument. We will suggest below that Peter's being an authority on the subject area in question would count as such evidence.

Using 'A' to stand for any person and 'p' to stand for any statement, we would not accept the following as a good argument:

> A asserts p.
> Therefore: p is true.                                    (argument A1)

Nevertheless, we do need to be able to make judgements as to whether or not a person's statements can be relied on. Another way of putting this point is that we need to know whether or not a particular person is a reliable authority on what we need to know. How would we go about judging whether or not this is the case?

No one is infallible; we all make mistakes of fact at one time or another. Therefore, this version of the argument from authority will be unsound in all cases. Some people would argue that as it stands it is not really an argument at all since all it does is to back up the assertion that p is true with the further statement that A has asserted it. Adding the premiss: 'Nearly everything that A asserts is true' to the argument strengthens it slightly:

> Nearly everything that A asserts is true.
> A asserts p.
> Therefore: p is true.                                    (argument A2)

Notice that we are here dealing with an *inductive* argument.

Notice that if the first premiss were: 'Everything A asserts is true' the argument would become a *deductive* one:

Everything that A asserts is true.
A asserts p.
Therefore: p is true.                                    (argument A3)

*Exercise*
Why would it become deductive? Notice also that it is an argument which, although valid, is unlikely to prove anything. Why is this?

The argument becomes deductive because the first premiss has become a universal statement. Though valid it is unlikely to prove anything because it is unlikely to be the case that everything that A says is true.

Our inductive argument about A (argument A2), although sound, is not of any more practical use than the deductive argument just given (argument A3). It is simply not true of any of us that nearly everything that we say is true. Even if we are not telling lies all the time, we are certainly making mistakes, particularly when we pronounce on matters about which we know very little. The most we can say with confidence about anyone is that there is some restricted area of knowledge about which the person is a reliable authority. We might now have:

Nearly everything A says about subject s is true.
p is a statement made by A about subject s.
Therefore: p is true.                                    (argument A4)

This is an argument from authority and it is sound because it gives good grounds for believing that p is true, given the truth of the premisses.
There are ways in which the argument from authority can be misused. The most obvious way in which it can be misused is for A to be an accepted authority on s but for her to pronounce in an authoritative way on a subject that is not s. In order to be sound, the argument from authority has got to be used in a way that is sensitive to the boundaries of competence of the authority in question. The following is, therefore, an unsound form of the argument from authority:

Nearly everything A says about subject s is true.
p is a statement made by A (p is about subject t).
Therefore: p is true.                                    (argument A5)

It is very tempting for an authority to pronounce or to be persuaded to pronounce outside his area of competence. In addition to the respect that they enjoy as experts in their chosen field, authorities very often carry an aura of *mystique* about them which may incline people to believe what they say even when there are no rational grounds for doing so. When authorities capitalize on this by pronouncing on issues about which they are legitimately considered as authorities they are clearly attempting non-rational persuasion in the sense in which this was introduced in Section 3.1. The authority relies on the admiration, respect or devotion she evokes in respect of her expertise in a particular field, in order to win assent for statements not backed up with good reasons or evidence in another field. The philosopher Bertrand Russell, who was a leading figure in the field of mathematical logic and epistemology but who also wrote widely on marriage, war and education could be considered a writer whose authority in one field gave him a prestige in other fields which was not really matched by his expertise in those other fields. You may recognize this technique as it is commonly applied by advertisers who often pay some famous personality to endorse the product which they wish to sell.

A second way in which arguments from authority can be problematic is when there is a genuine dispute between authorities within a particular field of competence. It may be the case that most or nearly all of what A says about s is true. However, B may be an authority about s as well and assert that not-p, while A asserts that p. How is the audience to decide between the two, particularly if they have little or no competence in the subject in question? It may be impossible to come to a rational decision in many cases. However, it would be a mistake to believe one authority rather than another simply because of her greater prestige, popularity, fluency, plausibility or charisma. This would be a mistake similar to the one illustrated in the unsound argument from authority above where it was assumed that A's being an authority on subject s gave her the right to pronounce on subject t.

We have discussed some of the problems that arise in the use of arguments from authority. One should also be aware of the distinction between being *an authority* and being *in authority*. Someone may be an authority on medicine, for example, because of her acknowledged expertise in the field. She may also be a senior figure in a medical institution, such as a hospital. Although many people who are authorities in their subjects are also *in* authority in their profession or institution, their being *in* authority does not make them *an* authority. It may even be possible to abuse one's position of being in authority to bolster one's prestige as an authority. An example might be an indolent university professor who achieves fame by requiring that all publications by her postgraduate students contain her name as first author.

Authorities in dispute with one another will have to deploy arguments in support of their own positions and in criticism of those with whom they disagree. In doing so they will allow the possibility of evaluation of their own arguments by others. Most often it will be difficult for someone without *any* knowledge of the subject specialist area to make a judgement as to the cogency of these arguments. But someone with a reasonable background knowledge of an area will be able to evaluate arguments. She will be able to note unstated premisses and form these, together with stated premisses and intermediate steps, into more fully articulated arguments. She will also be able to form judgements as to the likely truth or falsity of premisses in arguments used. A degree of expertise, however achieved, gives one a right to form judgements about disagreements between authorities. Where an authority uses an argument which is explicitly articulated and clearly invalid or unsound, the thoughtful non-expert should be in a position to make a judgement about the quality of the argument without knowing very much about the subject matter. The point to remember is that while we should maintain a proper respect for individual expertise and the complexity of particular subject matters, we do not have to surrender our rational faculties in situations where it is still possible to form judgements on the evidence and arguments available.

## Dealing with arguments and disagreements in what you read

You need to be sure that you understand the arguments and evidence that are being deployed in favour of different points of view in what you read. A good way of helping you with this is to make notes on relevant passages which actually try to set out the arguments put forward in as explicit a manner as possible. This may mean inserting what you take to be unstated intermediate steps and premisses in order to obtain the best possible construction of what you think different authors are trying to say. This is a theme to which we will return in the next section.

# 3.3 Analysing and evaluating arguments

A contrast is often made between two sorts of criminal justice system. One, typified by judicial practice in the United Kingdom and the United States, is *adversarial*. Trials are seen as a contest between the defence and the prosecution, the object of the trial being to produce a victory for the case which is most convincing. The prosecution needs to overcome the presumption of innocence on the part of the defendant, the defence to maintain that presumption. The other, typified by the French system of justice, is *inquistorial*. Here the object of a trial is to determine what actually occurred, that is, whether or not the crime actually took place at the time and place alleged.

Without pushing the parallel too far, it is possible to look at the evaluation of arguments from an adversarial or an inquisitorial point of view. We might, for example, think of the evaluation of arguments as a kind of contest, where the object of the reader or the interlocutor is to show the writer to have used an unsound argument of one kind or another. Alternatively, we might adopt something like the inquisitorial approach, where the object of the reader is to discover what the author actually meant by what she wrote, even if her meaning or argumentation is obscure or ambiguous. We are going to argue for the inquisitorial approach (without, however, expressing any preferences for one sort of legal system or another), when reading and evaluating the arguments of an author. However, unlike the French system of justice, in which the accused is presumed to be guilty until found to be innocent, we are going to recommend that the burden of proving that the author is 'guilty' of using a bad argument is up to the reader or critic. If the reader fails to do so, we suggest that the author should be assumed to have argued well. In other words, while we suggest that you should be careful and thorough in your evaluation of the arguments used by an author, you should also be prepared to try to understand her on her own terms and to offer a sympathetic interpretation of what she meant.

## Criticizing others is not a blood sport

In their book, *Philosophizing about Education* Straughan and Wilson (1983) undertake to show students how to philosophize. Their intentions are good. However, some of the practices that they demonstrate would, if taken up by a novice, lead to a cast of mind in the reader such that he looked only for faults, ambiguities and omissions, in order to show the writer to be muddled and incompetent. We recommend that you avoid this approach in your own writing. Scholarship is not, or at least should not be, a form of blood sport. The first business of the reader is to try and understand what is going on in a passage, *then* to subject it to measured evaluation.

Here is an example of the way in which Straughan and Wilson adopt an adversarial approach which goes out of its way to present the position criticized in a harsh and unsympathetic light. They present for evaluation the following passage from *Future Shock*, by Alvin Toffler:

> What passes for education today, even in our 'best' schools and colleges, is a hopeless anachronism. Parents look to education to fit their children for life in the future. Teachers warn that lack of an education will cripple a child's chances in the world of tomorrow. Government ministries, churches, the mass media – all exhort young people to stay in school, insisting that now, as never before, one's future is almost wholly dependent upon education.
>
> Yet for all this rhetoric about the future, our schools face backward towards a dying system, rather than forward to the emerging new society. Their vast energies are applied to cranking out Industrial men – people tooled for survival in a system that will be dead before they are.
>
> To help avert future shock, we must create a super-industrial education system. And to do this, we must search for our objectives and methods in the future rather than the past.
>
> (Toffler 1970, pp. 353–4, cited in Straughan and Wilson 1983)

Straughan and Wilson do not waste much time before showing students how to dissect this passage; their intention is to demonstrate that it shows a total muddle on Toffler's part. They write:

> To begin with, this author does not seem to have thought about the concept of education at all, and in particular about its central concern with the development of knowledge and understanding.
>
> (Straughan and Wilson 1983, p. 21)

Aren't Straughan and Wilson being a bit tough on Toffler here? We cannot infer from this passage that he has not thought about education at all. What would give us the right to say that? Adopting the inquisitorial approach would lead us to take him at face value as someone who is trying to make sense to his readers. Taking this more generous approach would lead us to consider the possibility that he simply has a different conception of education from that of Straughan and Wilson. He may have more than one conception of education. We are not entitled to assume at the outset that there is one conception of education and then use this as a yardstick against which to measure everyone else's. Moreover, it is far from clear that

Toffler does not consider the development of knowledge and understanding to be central to education. He certainly does not say anything like that in the passage just cited. Neither can one infer it from what he has written. One may indeed *suspect* it, as Straughan and Wilson clearly do, but those are not good grounds for asserting such a strong view without further evidence.

The reader needs to understand what Toffler's conception of education is before he can subject it to any sort of evaluation or criticism. Focusing on an isolated passage out of context will not allow her to do this. On the other hand, looking at the book as a whole, or at least, at its relevant chapters and passages will provide the basis for such an assessment. We cannot criticize if we do not know what we are criticizing or if we do not properly understand it. Since we are unfamiliar with Toffler's book we cannot tell whether Straughan and Wilson's conclusions about his view of education are based upon this one passage or on a wider reading of the book. If it is based on this single passage then they stand accused of a lack of generosity in the way in which they present his views; certainly as we have said, it is not possible to infer from this passage that Toffler has failed to think about education as deeply as he might have done. If their interpretation of Toffler's view is based on a wider reading then they have simply been unwise in talking as if it is possible to infer from this passage more than one can legitimately infer from it. In either case their selection of this passage does not give their own readers grounds for believing what they assert about Toffler's views of education.

## Being your own most rigorous critic

So far we have been suggesting that in evaluating the writing of others it is likely to be more productive to adopt a generous inquisitorial approach in which the task in hand is to try to understand what the writer is trying to say. On the other hand, when one is evaluating what one has written oneself, it pays to be one's own severest critic, thus ensuring that the highest standards of evaluation are applied to one's own work. In this case, we suggest that the author adopts an adversarial approach to his own writing. Alternatively, as we argued for strongly in Part 2, one can ask a trusted friend or colleague to adopt such a stance on occasion.

Why this use of different standards when reading one's own and other people's work? When one is reading an author, usually one is trying to understand what she says, even if one feels oneself to be in disagreement. Indeed, it can be argued that one needs to understand what someone is saying properly before one can apply any form of criticism to it.

However, when you are *writing* for an audience, it is necessary to provide your readership with as clear as possible a statement of your case if you wish to be understood. Remember what we wrote in Part 1 about the peculiar demands of written as opposed to spoken communication. You are writing for a non-present audience, maybe an unknown audience, who cannot interact with or question you. This involves thinking yourself into the place of the reader. You can do this most effectively, we believe, if you get into the habit of subjecting your own writing to adversarial criticism. What we are really suggesting is that you test your own writing for readability, relevance, fairness and consistency before you submit it to a wider audience.

## Evaluating your own work

Here are some of the main points that you should look for in evaluating your own work.

(i)   Have you written in clear, accessible and unambiguous prose, eliminating jargon and cliché whenever possible? Refer back to Part 2 if you need further guidance on this matter.

(ii)  If you are in any way reporting or evaluating what someone else has said or written, do you understand what they are saying? If what they are saying is ambiguous have you at least alerted your readers to that possibility? Obviously you cannot report all that they say or write, but have you given a fair and comprehensive account of what they say in terms of the task that you have set yourself?

(iii) This point is closely related to the last. Are you being fair in your representation of others' points of view. Are you sure that you are not distorting what they are trying to say? It may be necessary to check back to the original text if you are not completely sure about this. If you are quoting someone, does the passage you use actually reflect the point that you wish to make about what the author is saying? Have you quoted the relevant passage properly without omitting key words or phrases that would drastically alter the sense of what is being said by the author? For example, an author might write:

> I am committed to the benefits of education being made available to all children, including the very gifted. I do not consider education to be the sole preserve of those who need careful and deliberate instruction.

If one were careless or unscrupulous, a bit of judicious cutting could leave the author appearing to write:

> I am committed to the benefits of education being made available to the very gifted. I do not consider education to be the preserve of those who need careful and deliberate instruction.

. This may seem like a particularly blatant distortion, like those theatre banners which read '"A Marvellous Evening" . . . *Toytown Theatre News*', which, when you look up the full quotation, might read something like: 'Watching this play was for me most definitely not a marvellous evening'. However, harmful misquotation is easily done through haste, carelessness or over-anxiety to establish one's own position even by those who have no desire to mislead. Remember that even the omission of a word, particularly a word like 'not' from a sentence, can completely alter its sense.

(iv) Using the conventions for citation and bibliographical references that we outline in Section 2.10, have you ensured that your readers have the opportunity to check that you have been accurate in the presentation of other authors' arguments and contentions?

(v) Finally, what about your own argumentation? Are you being consistent? Have you contradicted yourself anywhere in the text? Even if you have not done so explicitly is it possible to deduce any contradictions from inconsistent views which you have expressed in different parts of your text? Make sure that you understand the nature of the arguments that you are using and then ask yourself whether they are sound or unsound. Are you in fact totally committed to the business of rational persuasion or have you fallen prey to the temptation to use rhetorical or indoctrinatory techniques such as were described in Section 3.1?

## Other people's arguments

So far in this section we have discussed the differences between an adversarial and a generously inquisitorial approach to evaluating what people have to say. Whereas we have advocated the adoption of the inquisitorial approach to what other people write, we have suggested that it would be in your best interests to adopt a more adversarial approach to assessing what you have written yourself. We now want to focus on the evaluation of other people's arguments. By looking at some extended examples we hope to give you practice in the skill of assessing arguments including, for example, working out *what* is being argued for and *whether* the argument is sound.

In Part 1 we discussed some of the distinctions between the presentation of thoughts and arguments in speech and in writing. For example, we pointed out that whereas in speech there is most often the possibility of direct interaction between speaker and listener which allows for the gradual elaboration of one's position, in writing this possibility does not exist. When one is writing one has to take greater care in the presentation, development and justification of one's position.

Let us look at a few examples in which an attempt is being made to argue in favour of a point of view; each of these forms the basis of an extended exercise. First of all, let us consider an example drawn from speech. Naturally enough, following the ins and outs of a conversation can be confusing, particularly if one is trying to pick out the arguments that are being developed. Bear in mind that this is a somewhat simple example, since only one argument is expressed, while in a genuine disagreement both parties are advancing arguments which are often opposed to each other.

*Exercise 1*

In the following conversation which is based on an example taken from William Labov (1969), two people, C.R. and Larry, are having a conversation about what might happen to people after they die.

C.R.: Have you ever thought about what happens to people when they die? I know you were told about it in Sunday School and so on, but I want to know about your own thoughts.

Larry: Well, I do have my own views on that.

C.R.: What are they then? I'm dying to know.

Larry: What I think is, when you die, your body just decomposes.

C.R.: So tell me something new. I thought you'd been thinking about this. I want to know what you think happens to your soul.

Larry: Your soul leaves you when you die.

C.R.: Where do you think it goes then?

Larry: Well, I'm not really sure about that . . .

C.R.: Come on, I thought you'd been giving this some thought.

Larry: OK. A lot of people still think that if you're good your soul goes to heaven and if you're bad your soul goes to hell. I think that's a load of rubbish, quite frankly. In the long run, we're all going to hell.

C.R.: I'm beginning to be sorry I asked you now! Whatever makes you think like that?

Larry: Look, nobody really knows if God exists. You know, I've travelled a bit in my time and I've seen more gods than you've had hot dinners. They can't all exist and I don't think that any of them exist. So when folk say if you're good, your soul will go to heaven, that's absolute rubbish because there isn't a heaven for it to go to. Good or bad, your soul is going to hell anyway.

*Questions*

Here are some questions designed to help you to come to an understanding of Larry's position. You should spend some time on them before reading our discussion of the example which follows.

(i) Is Larry developing an argument or arguments in the course of this conversation?

(ii) What are the conclusions of Larry's argument(s)?

(iii) What are the premises of Larry's argument or arguments?

(iv) Are there any ambiguous statements made in the course of these arguments?

(v) Set out the arguments that you think that Larry is developing, arranging them as sets of premises, intermediate steps (if you think that there are any) and conclusions, in that order. If you think they contain any premisses that are not made explicit, state what you think they are.

(vi)   Are the arguments developed by Larry good?

*Discussion of questions*

(i)    Larry is developing two arguments.
(ii)   There are two conclusions. One is the conclusion that it's absolute rubbish to say that if you're good your soul is going to heaven and if you're bad your soul is going to hell. The other conclusion is that, good or bad, your soul is going to hell.
(iii)  The premisses of the first argument are:
   (a)  There is no heaven for your soul to go to.
   (b)  It is absolute rubbish that if you are good your soul will go to heaven. (This follows from premiss (a); strictly speaking it is an intermediate step.)
   (c)  If you're good, your soul goes to heaven and if you're bad your soul goes to hell. (This is an unstated premiss that is supposed in the course of the first argument.)
   The second argument has one premiss which is:

   In the long run, we're all going to hell.

(iv)   We don't think so but some people might. They might think that Larry's statement: 'A lot of people still think that if you're good your soul goes to heaven and if you're bad you're soul goes to hell. I think that's a load of rubbish, quite frankly.' is ambiguous. They might think that it is ambiguous because they think it is unclear whether Larry intends to say that both the idea that *if you're good your soul is going to heaven* is rubbish and the idea that *if you're bad your soul is going to hell* is rubbish, or rather that *if you're good your soul is going to heaven and if you're bad your soul is going to hell* is rubbish.
(v)    First argument:
   (a)  There is no heaven for your soul to go to. (premiss)
   (b)  It is absolute rubbish that if you are good your soul will go to heaven. (intermediate step)
   (c)  If you're good, your soul goes to heaven and if you're bad your soul goes to hell. (second, unstated premiss which is *supposed*, for the sake of the argument but not asserted)
   (d)  If you're good, then your soul goes to heaven. (intermediate step which follows from (c))
   (e)  If you're good, then your soul goes to heaven and it is rubbish that if you're good your soul goes to heaven. (intermediate step obtained by joining together (b) and (d))
   (f)  Therefore: It is rubbish that if you're good your soul goes to heaven and if you're bad your soul goes to hell. (conclusion)
   The conclusion to the argument is obtained by denying the premiss

that was supposed for the sake of the argument (c). This can be done because supposing (c) has led to (e) which cannot be true.

Second argument:

> In the long run we're all going to hell.
>
> Therefore: Good or bad, your soul is going to hell.

(vi) We think that both arguments are good arguments. However, someone who thought that Larry was being ambiguous in the way described in our discussion of question (iv) might argue that Larry's first argument was a bad one and that Larry was a muddled rather than an astute thinker. If you are interested in reading about why they might conclude this, you may care to look at what William Labov (1969) and David Cooper (1984) have to say about this example.

It is easy to see how different the argument looks now that it has been set out explicitly in contrast to the fragmentary and implicit form that it took in the conversation between Larry and C.R. Our discussion of this conversation illustrates how important it is to state clearly what you wish to say and to set out any argument that you are putting forward as clearly as you can. Of course, it is much more difficult to do this in the context of a conversation such as that between Larry and C.R. than when we are constructing a written argument. Larry can hardly be blamed for failing to state his argument clearly and without ambiguity as the conversation in which he puts forward his argument is not a situation over which he has full control. Larry is engaged in a competitive battle of wits. As a writer, on the other hand, you do not face these constraints, although you do face others. As a writer you can state your argument clearly and without ambiguity and you must do so if you wish to get your message across in the form in which you wish your readership to receive it.

No author can hope to include 'll the possible premises of her arguments. Neither can she hope to provide arguments for the truth of all her premises. She must, therefore, take into account the knowledge and assumptions that her readership might reasonably be expected to have. This background of knowledge and assumptions will vary according to the readership in question: whether or not it is a general or specialized audience, its degree of education, and its willingness to give sympathetic attention to her views. When this has been done, the writer must ensure that her arguments are not ambiguous for other reasons, for instance because she has omitted crucial intervening steps.

A writer has the opportunity and responsibility to maximize clarity and eliminate ambiguity. It is helpful if at the outset of a piece of writing which is going to serve as an argument for a certain position, the author makes a clear statement of the conclusion she is attempting to establish. Let us take one last look at Larry's argument. How might he go about presenting it in writing if by now he has had some lessons in the clear presentation of arguments? He might begin by stating:

> I am going to argue that the view that the souls of good people go to heaven and the souls of bad people go to hell when they die, is false.

This statement would focus the reader clearly on the aim of what was to follow. Next Larry would have to state clearly the premises on which he is basing this argument. He might begin by supposing that the view which he is arguing against, is true:

> Suppose, for the sake of the argument, that if you are good your soul goes to heaven and if you are bad your soul goes to hell.

The concealed premiss in his original argument is thus made explicit. The next premiss in his argument can now be introduced and if that itself follows from a previous argument this can be made clear.

> Now, it is false that if you are good then your soul is going to heaven, since there is no heaven and you cannot go somewhere which does not exist.

The premiss 'It is false that if you are good then your soul is going to heaven' is thus supported by a smaller argument.

Larry has now supposed one premiss for the sake of argument and argued in favour of another:

> If you are good your soul goes to heaven and if you're bad your soul goes to hell.
> It is false that if you are good then your soul is going to heaven.

But these two premisses implicitly contradict one another and so Larry will have to point this out:

> Given the truth of my earlier supposition, it follows that if you are good then your soul is going to heaven. However, I have just argued that it is false that if you are good then your soul is going to heaven.

Finally, since it is not possible for both these statements to be true Larry can reject the supposition that if you are good then your soul will go to heaven and if you are bad your soul will go to hell:

> It can, therefore, be concluded that the statement that if you are good then your soul is going to heaven and if you are bad then your soul is going to hell, is false.

Larry has thus clearly stated his argument.

*Exercise 2*

The following is an article from the *Guardian* giving its author's strong views about teachers. Read it and make an assessment of it as a piece of persuasion. Does it contain any arguments or is it merely a collection of persuasive assertions and opinions? You should pay particular attention to the use of rhetorical devices such as the use of persuaders, emotive language, or illicit appeals to authority which are employed to nudge the reader in the direction of agreement with the views of the writer. Do ensure that you try to make sympathetic sense of what the author is arguing before you decide (if indeed you do) to criticize the arguments employed.

### I Blame the Teachers

Not a day goes by without the usual media headlines informing us of yet more disquieting facts and figures on football hooliganism, drug abuse, child sexual abuse, muggings, rapings and murder. But whenever I hear of a criminal brought to justice I always feel the real criminals go free. Who do I mean? I mean the teaching profession. They know that hidden in their well protected ranks are the people who regularly criminalise the next generation. Not many people will agree with this philosophy but personal experience has reinforced it for me time and time again.

If a child comes into school at the tender age of five or less, from a deprived home with socially inadequate parents schooling will do nothing for him. Indeed it will often exacerbate his problems. Very soon a psychologically unsound teacher will use that child as a scapegoat – the means of keeping the rest of the class in order despite their boredom.

I know this because I've been a scapegoat (although my home wasn't deprived and my parents were socially adequate). I know this because my three children were always in classes where it happened. I know this because my husband was a schoolteacher until utter disillusionment made him throw in the towel. Ask any individual and they can all name a scapegoat, from their schooldays. Ask any individual teacher and they will admit it privately: 'of course it goes on' they say, 'but what can I do about it?' they plead.

I also have written evidence in my postbag every day of the week. Working for an educational organisation is heartrending work. The stories of scapegoating and humiliation in our schools make dreadful daily reading.

... Now, years later, the children that my children saw beaten, humiliated, ridiculed and generally demoralised make news in the local newspapers as thieves, drunks and general hellraisers. They are, of course, punished but the real criminals are still highly respected members of the community and no doubt continue to criminalise their present disadvantaged pupils as do so many members of the highly protected teaching profession. As I said, the real criminals go free. And I say it on behalf of all those who aren't free to do so.

(Janet Everdell, *Guardian*, 30 September 1986, p. 11, column 1)

### Discussion

There is an argument, albeit rather a weak one, which reaches a number of conclusions which are difficult to state clearly but which certainly include the idea that teachers are responsible for most of the crime that occurs in society from football hooliganism, child sexual abuse, muggings and rapings to murder, and furthermore that teachers themselves are criminals because of their part in the creation of the criminals who perpetrate such crimes. The premisses are too numerous to mention but include, for example, 'some teachers regularly criminalise the next generation'. 'If a child comes into school . . . from a deprived home with socially inadequate parents schooling will do nothing for him', and 'such a child will be used as a scapegoat by a psychologically unsound teacher'. It is difficult to use the author's own words to state the premisses but these have been stated using as many as possible of the author's own words. (Do you think we have been fair in our statement of them?) In addition there are many hidden or suppressed premisses including, for example, 'Children who are ill treated mostly turn into criminals' and 'The psychological damage teachers do to pupils is more important than any other experiences they have in forming the character of those pupils who go on to become criminals'.

This example presents instances of several of the dubious moves that we examined in Section 3.2. You should have spotted examples of emotional content ('working for an educational organisation is heartrending work'); rash generalizations ('I always feel the real criminals go free'); an illegitimate appeal to authority (what is the nature of the educational organization for which the author works and how does her work qualify her to pronounce on matters of educational discipline?); the use of limited evidence (the postbag, her own children's experiences); the 'you're not going to believe this' move ('Not many people will agree with this philosophy but personal experience has reinforced it for me time and time again').

Having spent some time on this example, you may care to examine now a piece of anecdotal evidence that comprised part of the original article which we give below. Ask yourself whether this additional material, which cites empirical though rather limited evidence, would make any difference to your assessment of the argument. For example, would *it* lead you to 'Blame the Teachers'?

One progressive teacher I know was working in a comprehensive school where some of his first year boy pupils confided in him that they were being corporally punished during PE lessons. They would be hit on the backside with a table tennis bat for being last to change their clothing or last in any race that took place during the PE lesson. The teacher told his union and the LEA. The LEA said it was not a matter for them, it was for the headmaster. The union and the headmaster reprimanded the teacher for unprofessional behaviour towards a colleague.

The teacher persisted on behalf of the children claiming they had a legitimate grievance as they were receiving illegal corporal punishment and none of it was being entered in the punishment book.

How, the teacher asked all those in authority, would the children be able to grow up with a sense of justice? He never got an answer. They all mumbled lame excuses like 'It's only a bit of fun' – 'It's only a bit of rough and tumble' – 'It knocks the raw edges off them' – 'It's common practice in boys' PE'.

In order to keep his job the teacher was forced to write an apology to the PE master concerned. Nevertheless, eighteen months later he found himself dismissed on charges of incompetence and refusal to obey the headmaster's orders. It didn't appear to concern anyone that the teacher claimed the headmaster's orders were immoral and therefore against his principles.

During his last months at the school the braver members of staff confided in him saying things like 'I know what you're trying to do but you're before our time', or 'I can't risk what you're doing – I've got a mortgage'.

(Everdell, op. cit.)

*Exercise 3*

It has been argued by Cooper (1984), that Charles M., who was quoted on pages 37–8, can be seen as presenting a coherent argument, if the appropriate concealed premiss is made clear. Here, again, is the passage from Charles as cited by Labov (1969):

Well, I even heard my parents say that there is such a thing as something in dreams some things like that, and sometimes dreams do come true. I have personally never had a dream come true. I've never dreamt that somebody was dying and they actually died, or that I was going to have ten dollars the next day and somehow I got ten dollars in my pocket. I don't particularly believe in that, I don't think it's true. I do feel, though that there is such a thing as – ah – witchcraft. I do feel that in certain cultures there is such a thing as witchcraft, or some sort of *science* of witchcraft; I don't think that it's just a matter of believing hard enough that there is such a thing as witchcraft. I do believe that there is such a thing that a person can put himself in a state of *mind*, or that – er – something could be given them to intoxicate them in a certain – to – to a certain frame of mind – that – that could actually be considered witchcraft.

(pp. 197–8)

*Questions*

(i)   What is Charles's conclusion?
(ii)  What are the premises, stated or unstated, on which his argument rests?
(iii) Set out the argument in a clear and unambiguous way, similar to the

recasting of Larry's argument about heaven and hell which we gave above.

*Discussion*

This example *looks* much less coherent than the heaven and hell example, but this is not necessarily because the thinking behind the statements is much less coherent. There is a lot of hesitation, there is repetition, and there appear to be great gaps in the main argument. Since we cannot interrogate Charles it is not possible for us to say whether or not he was aware of or would be able to supply the missing premisses that would make his argument more convincing. Filling in some of the possible unstated premisses, Charles could be seen as offering a valid argument as outlined below:

(i)    The conclusion is: 'I don't believe that dreams come true'.

(ii)   There are three premisses, two of which are unstated:

> In all matters of the supernatural, personal experience is the only criterion for belief. (unstated premiss)

> Dreams that come true are an example of supernatural matters. (unstated premiss)

> I have never had personal experience of a dream coming true. (stated premiss)

(iii)  Taking these stated and unstated premisses we can construct the following valid argument:

(a)  In all matters of the supernatural, personal experience is the only criterion for belief. (unstated premiss)

(b)  Dreams that come true are an example of supernatural matters. (unstated premiss)

(c)  The only criterion for believing that dreams come true is by having personal experience of dreams coming true. (intermediate step, from (a) and (b))

(d)  I have never had personal experience of a dream coming true.

(e)  Therefore I don't believe that dreams come true.

Given the information we have about what Charles thinks and the impossibility of gaining any further information about his thinking, this seems to be a sympathetic interpretation of his position which is quite consistent with what we know him to have asserted.

# Postscript

If you are reading this postscript you have probably done at least one of several things. You may be reading it because you're just at the end of reading the book from cover to cover in the hope of finding some tips that will help you when you are writing as a student. If this is the case we hope you have found something that is of value to you; if not we suggest that you re-read Section 1.2 because you could do with learning how to assess whether a book is worth reading from cover to cover. Or perhaps you are reading it for the same reason that you have already cast your eye briefly over the contents page, index and introduction – to gain some impression of what the book is about in order to decide whether it is worth buying it or taking out of the library. If this is so you can congratulate yourself on having at least one good reading habit; we hope that you gain the impression that at least some of what we say will be worth reading in detail. Finally, you may be reading this postscript in detail because you noticed that in the preface we invited readers to inform us of mistakes we have made – of places where we fail to heed advice we have offered – and you hope to cash in on your ability as a proof-reader. If this is the case we hope that reading the postscript proves a sterile exercise.

Let us, by way of some concluding remarks, briefly remind you of some of the main points that we have tried to make. We wrote *Reading, Writing and Reasoning* because our experience of teaching at undergraduate level suggested that students often lack many of the literary skills that are necessary if they are to make efficient use of written materials and, perhaps even more importantly, if they are to be successful in their own writing. It also seemed to us that they often have very little idea about what it is to offer arguments in the form of reasons and/or evidence, in support of the points of view that they wish to support, other than by referring to other writers.

The book is divided into three parts. Part 1 makes some points about the difference between written and spoken communication and discusses the nature of reading and writing. Part 2 offers some simple advice about how you might make your own writing as effective as possible. Finally, Part 3 discusses the distinction that is to be made between rational and other forms of persuasion and gives some practice in the construction and analysis of arguments.

A continuing theme in the book has been the need to be continually aware of the differences that exist between written and spoken communication and to keep in mind the needs of the audience for whom one is writing. Whereas when we are speaking, our audience can ask for clarification, or amplification in the case of a complex argument with many hidden premisses or intermediate steps, when we are writing this possibility does not exist. So we argued, it is essential when you are writing that you think carefully about what is essential and what inessential to the points you are trying to make. This is probably the most important point we make in Part 1 and it impinges upon much of Part 2 in which, among other things, we sought to emphasize the fact that successful writing is not easy and requires a great deal of commitment on the part of a writer.

In Part 2 we discussed a range of writing skills including such basics as punctuation, spelling, the accurate citation of references, and attending closely to the purpose you have in writing. We also discussed higher-order skills such as attending to the way in which you structure what you write, developing an awareness of the importance of style, and carefully drafting and revising so that you ensure that your essays succeed in saying what you want to say effectively and efficiently.

In Part 3 we distinguished between arguing in favour of a point of view and merely asserting it. After a discussion of the difference between rational and non-rational means of persuasion we offered practice in the evaluation and construction of arguments and in spotting examples of non-rational persuasion. We argued in favour of an approach to reading that is generous and inquisitorial rather than destructive both because adopting such an approach can help you to develop your own writing skills and because it can help you to make the best use possible of the time you spend reading. Notice, however, that in promoting a generously critical approach to reading texts we do not wish to give the impression that you should accept everything that you read; indeed we have warned against coming to believe everything that published authors have written, even when they are acknowledged authorities in relation to some area of human knowledge and experience.

We hope that as a result of reading the book you will become better at reading, writing and reasoning; we hope also that you will come to enjoy your work more than you did previously. If you change the way you think about what you read and write in the kinds of ways we have suggested and adopt some of the approaches we have described we think that this will happen. However, it is likely also that you will become less pleased with your writing. We have argued in favour of measuring your work against the highest possible standards of self-criticism. As a result you may find it less easy to satisfy yourself in future; this is all to the good, provided you remember that even professional writers find it difficult to satisfy themselves. With the best will in the world you are unlikely ever to satisfy all the various demands that may be made on what you write. But part of the business of growing up as a writer, as we argued in Part 2, is that you should take responsibility for what you write and this means that at a certain point in writing whatever it is that you have to write, you have to decide that you cannot do any better – this time. As a general rule, however, you should not expect to complete a final version of a dissertation or project report without having written and revised several drafts first. Essays may require fewer drafts but you should expect to revise them at least once.

There is a great deal of satisfaction to be gained from seeing yourself become more skilled as a writer. We can all improve all the time. While writing this book, for example, we noticed many times how deficient our own skills seemed to be; hence our invitation to readers to point out places where we have made mistakes! Do not be afraid of using friends and fellow students for mutual support as readers and commentators on your work. Though difficult to stomach at times, the helpful and supportive criticisms of another can be invaluable in helping you to locate flaws in your arguments and in the way in which you have structured your work as well as flaws in your spelling. You will probably notice in scholarly articles and books that the author often thanks various people for help, comments and criticism. Sharing one's work with others is such a valuable practice that it is carried out at the most advanced levels of study.

If you have already read the book we hope you have enjoyed it and found it useful. If you have not yet read it we hope that you will do so. In any event the fact that you have at least thought about using a book like this means that you are taking seriously the need to think clearly and that you realize that writing is not an easy task. However, it is one that you can enjoy and by taking it seriously you can be sure that writing will become a more pleasurable experience.

# References

On page 67 we pointed out the conflict between the punctuation style we suggest you adopt in writing references and the 'house-style' of the Open University Press which appears here. At the risk of being boring it seems appropriate to point this out again to avoid the risk of confusion.

Abbs, P. (1987). Training spells the death of education, *Guardian*, 5 January.
Allen, E. V. (1977). *Logical Spelling*. London: Collins.
Barker-Lunn, J. (1970). *Streaming in the Primary School*. Slough: NFER.
Barrass, R. (1982). *Students Must Write*. London: Methuen.
Beard, R. (1987). *Developing Reading 3–13*. London: Hodder & Stoughton.
British Standards Institute (1978). *Citing Publications by Bibliographical References*. London: British Standards Institute.
Burton, S. H. (1982). *Mastering English Language*. London: Macmillan Education.
Cooper, D. (1984). Labov, Larry and Charles, *Oxford Review of Education*, 10, 2: 177–92.
de S Cameron, N. M. (1989). Embryos again, *Ethics and Medicine*, 5.2: 17.
De Leeuw, M. and De Leeuw, E. (1963). *Read Better, Read Faster*. Harmondsworth: Penguin.
DES and Welsh Office (1990). *English in the National Curriculum*. London: HMSO.
Everdell, J. (1986). I blame the teachers, *Guardian*, 30 September, p. 11, column 1.
Fairbairn, G. J. (1991). Enforced death: enforced life, *Journal of Medical Ethics*, 17.3.
Fisher Cassie, W. and Constantine, T. (1977). *Student's Guide to Success*. Basingstoke: Macmillan Education.
Flew, A. (1976). Academic freedoms and academic purposes. In Flew, A., *Sociology, Equality and Education*. London: Macmillan.
Fowler, H. W. (1965). *Dictionary of Modern English Usage*. Oxford: Clarendon Press.
Giglioli, P.-P. (ed.) (1972). *Language and Social Context*. Harmondsworth: Penguin.
Hanfling, O. (1978). *Uses and Abuses of Argument*, Course Units 2B and 9 for the course A101 an Arts Foundation Course, Milton Keynes: Open University.
Harris, J. (1975). The survival lottery, *Philosophy*, 50: 81–7.
Hart, H. L. A. (1966). *Punishment and Responsibility: Essays in the Philosophy of Law*. Oxford: Clarendon Press.
Hirsch, E. D. (1987). *Cultural Literacy. What Every American Should Know*. Boston: Houghton Mifflin.
Jaffrey, M. (1982). *Madhur Jaffrey's Indian Cookery*. London: BBC Publications.
Jehl, D. (1988). Family man Dan goes rambling for Thanksgiving, *Guardian*, 8 November, p. 24, column 7.
Labov, W. (1969). The logic of non-standard English. In Giglioli, P.-P. (ed.) (1972), *Language and Social Context*. Harmondsworth: Penguin.
Legat, M. (1989). *The Nuts and Bolts of Writing*. London: Robert Hale.

Luling, V. (1982). *Aborigines*. London: Macdonald.

Mair, J. M. M. (1970). Psychologists are human too. In Bannister, D. (ed.), *Perspectives in Personal Construct Theory*. London: Academic Press.

Mortimore, P., Sammons, P., Stoll, L. *et al.* (1988). *School Matters*. Wells, Somerset: Open Books.

Orwell, G. (1946). Politics and the English language. In *The Collected Essays, Journalism and Letters of George Orwell. Vol 4 – In Front of Your Nose* (1968). Harmondsworth: Penguin.

Oxford Paperback Dictionary (1988). Oxford: Oxford University Press.

Plato (undated). *Euthydemus*. In Hare, R. M. and Russell, D. A. (eds) (1970), *The Dialogues of Plato*, Vol. 2. London: Sphere.

Rawls, J. (1971). *A Theory of Justice*. Oxford: Oxford University Press.

Roget, P. M. (1962). *Roget's Thesaurus of English Words and Phrases*. Harlow: Longman.

Salmon, W. (1963). *Logic*. Englewood Cliffs, New Jersey: Prentice-Hall.

Shoosmith, H. (1928). *Spelling and Punctuation*. London: University Tutorial Press.

Shorter Oxford Dictionary (1973). Revised third edition. London: Oxford University Press.

Smith, H. (1981). *Strategies of Social Research: The Methodological Imagination*. Milton Keynes: Open University.

Straughan, R. and Wilson, J. (1983). *Philosophizing about Education*. London: Holt, Rinehart & Winston.

Tizard, B. and Hughes, M. (1984). *Young Children Learning*. London: Fontana.

Toffler, A. (1970). *Future Shock*. New York: Random House.

Vesey, G. (1974). *Philosophy in the Open*. Milton Keynes: Open University Press.

Wilson, J. (1973). *The Assessment of Morality*. Windsor: NFER.

Winch, C. (1985). Women, reason and education, *Journal of Philosophy of Education*, 19, 1: 95.

Wynne, P. (1985). Authority and the teacher. Unpublished BEd essay, NEWI, Cartrefle.

# Index

# The Society for Research into Higher Education

The Society for Research into Higher Education exists to stimulate and co-ordinate research into all aspects of higher education. It aims to improve the quality of higher education through the encouragement of debate and publication on issues of policy, on the organization and management of higher education institutions, and on the curriculum and teaching methods.

The Society's income is derived from subscriptions, sales of its books and journals, conference fees and grants. It receives no subsidies, and is wholly independent. Its individual members include teachers, researchers, managers and students. Its corporate members are institutions of higher education, research institutes, professional, industrial and governmental bodies. Members are not only from the UK, but from elsewhere in Europe, from America, Canada and Australasia, and it regards its international work as amongst its most important activities.

Under the imprint *SRHE & Open University Press*, the Society is a specialist publisher of research, having some 55 titles in print. The Editorial Board of the Society's Imprint seeks authoritative research or study in the above fields. It offers competitive royalties, a highly recognizable format in both hardback and paperback and the world-wide reputation of the Open University Press.

The Society also publishes *Studies in Higher Education* (three times a year), which is mainly concerned with academic issues, *Higher Education Quarterly* (formerly *Universities Quarterly*), mainly concerned with policy issues, *Research into Higher Education Abstracts* (three times a year), and *SRHE News* (four times a year).

The Society holds a major annual conference in December, jointly with an institution of higher education. In 1992, the topic was 'Learning to Effect' with Nottingham Trent University. In 1993, it was 'Governments and the Higher Education Curriculum: Evolving Partnerships' at the University of Sussex in Brighton, and in 1994, 'The Student Experience' at the University of York. Future conferences include in 1995, 'The Changing University' at Heriot-Watt University in Edinburgh.

The Society's committees, study groups and branches are run by the members. The groups at present include:

Teacher Education Study Group
Continuing Education Group
Staff Development Group
Excellence in Teaching and Learning

# Benefits to members

## *Individual*

Individual members receive:

- *SRHE News*, the Society's publications list, conference details and other material included in mailings.
- Greatly reduced rates for *Studies in Higher Education* and *Higher Education Quarterly*.
- A 35% discount on all Open University Press & SRHE publications.
- Free copies of the Precedings – commissioned papers on the theme of the Annual Conference.
- Free copies of *Research into Higher Education Abstracts*.
- Reduced rates for conferences.
- Extensive contacts and scope for facilitating initiatives.
- Reduced reciprocal memberships.

## *Corporate*

Corporate members receive:

- All benefits of individual members, plus
- Free copies of *Studies in Higher Education*.
- Unlimited copies of the Society's publications at reduced rates.
- Special rates for its members e.g. to the Annual Conference.

 *Membership details:* SRHE, 3 Devonshire Street, London, W1N 2BA, UK. Tel: 0171 637 2776
*Catalogue:* SRHE & Open University Press, Celtic Court, 22 Ballmoor, Buckingham MK18 1XW. Tel: (01280) 823388